S0-BEH-241

TO COMFORT AND TO HONOR

A Guide to Personalizing Rituals for the Passing of a Loved One

Jeanne Daly McIntee

Augsburg
MINNEAPOLIS

TO COMFORT AND TO HONOR
A Guide to Personalizing Rituals for the Passing of a Loved One

Copyright © 1998 Jeanne Daly McIntee. All rights reserved. Except for brief quotations in critical articles or reviews, no part of this book may be reproduced in any manner without prior written permission from the publisher. Write to: Permissions, Augsburg Fortress, Box 1209, Minneapolis, MN 55440.

Scripture passages are taken from the Holy Bible, New International Version, copyright © 1973, 1978, 1984 by International Bible Society. Used by permission of Zondervan Publishing House. All rights reserved.

The "NIV" and "New International Version" trademarks are registered in the United States Patent and Trademark Office by International Bible Society. Use of either trademark requires the permission of International Bible Society.

Excerpts from the English translation of *Pastoral Care of the Sick: Rites of Anointing and Viaticum* © 1982, International Committee on English in the Liturgy, Inc. (ICEL); excerpts from the English translation of Order of Christian Funerals © 1985, ICEL. All rights reserved.

From *Illuminata* by Marianne Williamson. Copyright © 1994 by Marianne Williamson. Reprinted by permission of Random House, Inc.

From *Jewish Insights on Death and Mourning*, edited by Jack Riemer. Copyright © 1995 by Jack Riemer. Reprinted with permission of Schocken Books, published by Pantheon Books, a division of Random House, Inc.

Some of the prayers in this book are from the *Lutheran Book of Worship* (Minneapolis: Lutheran Church in America, the American Lutheran Church, the Evangelical Lutheran Church in Canada, and the Lutheran Church-Missouri Synod, 1978).

Cover design by Barbara Beshoar and Marti Naughton.

Interior design by Jane Dahms.

Library of Congress Cataloging-in-Publication Data

McIntee, Jeanne Daly, 1958-
    To comfort and to honor : a guide to personalizing rituals for the passing of a loved one / Jeanne Daly McIntee
       p.   cm.
    Includes bibliographical references.
    ISBN 0-8066-3624-6 (alk. paper)
    1. Funeral rites and ceremonies—United States—Handbooks, manuals, etc.   I. Title.
    GT3203.M35   1998
    393—dc21
                                          98-19001
                                           CIP

The paper used in this publication meets the minimum requirements of American National Standard for Information Sciences—Permanence of Paper for Printed Library Materials, ANSI Z329.48-1984.

Manufactured in the U.S.A.   AF 9-3624

02   01   00   99   98   1   2   3   4   5   6   7   8   9   10

CONTENTS

In honor of those who go before us,

leaving memories which have helped to shape us,

reminding us that life is full of possibilities not yet seen.

ACKNOWLEDGMENTS

Grateful acknowlegment is given to the following individuals for their contributions of personal material used from the funerals of their loved ones: Caroline Abramson, Tyler McCabe, Jane Miller, J.M., and T.S.M.

To my husband, Tim, and children, Kate, Connor, Sean, and Maggie. Their love, patience, and support throughout this process helped me to stay the course.

I would like to thank the staff at Augsburg Books for their belief and commitment to this work. My thanks to Ronald Klug for his thoughtful editorial suggestions and Pamela Johnson for her unwavering support.

I thank Dr. Roberta Holt, Rabbi Barry Cytron, Father Patrick Lannon, Father Bill Baer, Dr. John Priest, Dr. Norman James, Sister Shaun O'Meara, Lynn Basich, and Kathy Hanousek for their thoughtful comments and suggestions. Appreciation is also extended to my family and friends, Angie, LuLu, Marie, Nancy, Gayle, Lois, and Jackie; my gratitude. Your help and comments during the writing and editing gave me the courage to continue. Barb and Jane, your skill and creative talents helped me to fulfill my dream.

PREFACE

I first began thinking about funeral rites out of need, much like anyone else. In 1984 my son's cancer relapsed and I was left to face the harsh reality that he would die before his first birthday. In my shock and sorrow I struggled to find a focus, something I could do to manage my feelings of loss and helplessness. The relapse of the cancer signaled the reality of his eventual death. I had prepared for his birth, and now I tried to find a way to prepare for his death. Having a task to complete is generally helpful in reestablishing some kind of balance, helping to integrate the incomprehensible into reality, and making the shock more manageable. For me, simply waiting for death to come was definitely not manageable.

I was fortunate to have had three months to prepare for his death. It gave me time to think about what it would mean, what I wanted to do, and how to live in the shadow of death. If I chose, I had some time to plan and prepare for his death. I did not know how to prepare for his death. Planning his funeral gave me a framework for how to do that.

Death was inevitable. Eventually I would be forced to face the funeral. I chose sooner, and found that each decision—which funeral home to use, where to bury him, what kind of flowers I wanted—helped me to accept what I could not change. For me, the task of handling the details involved was easier than looking at the big picture of death. I talked with my husband and a few close friends about the preparations I had undertaken. The communications were not frequent or long, just enough to ask for help with something specific or to get assistance sorting out the information I was getting.

What I discovered in my search for direction was that very little reference material focused specifically on the funeral ritual. There are many resources available for living with terminal illness, coping with loss, or living with grief after a death occurs. I found nothing that would give me a framework to use as a guide in planning my son's funeral. Like many people, I had been taught certain religious practices, but I was looking for something beyond the mechanics of a service. There was a great need to find a way to express the meaning of my experience with him. Part of my motivation was the desire to make sure I had done all I could for him. Some illnesses are a slow introduction to the realities of death. For many others, the experience comes through a sudden traumatic accident or event, or through unexpected or unexplained illness. The circumstances differ with each life.

There are many books available that provide thought material about these issues. You will find a short list of these in the bibliography. This guide is intended to help address the need and use of rituals in the time before death and after the death occurs.

HOW TO USE THIS GUIDE

When we live with a terminal illness or condition, it is difficult to find a way to accept the eventual death of a loved one. We struggle to think about how to care for the dying and to make the time together meaningful for each of us. Most of us are not prepared for the death of a loved one. We cope because we have to and because we can.

Much of the difficulty with facing death and funerals comes from our discomfort, feeling helpless or feeling at a loss for words or ideas about what to do. Planning for the funeral, before or after the death occurs, gives all of us the opportunity to speak about the unspeakable. The details provide the content for discussions and conversation, a specific focus in which we talk about death and dying, a topic that we normally avoid. In a sense, what once seemed horrific becomes commonplace for a while. This guide is offered as a service to you in difficult days.

Chapters 1 and 2 explore the impact of the time before death and the experience of being with someone when they die. Examples of and thoughts about the use of ceremony or ritual as a way to help us accept what we cannot change are presented. Questions are provided to help you think about how you may want to use this time. Chapters 3 through 8 address the issues and details that must be taken care of when planning a funeral service. Checklists, questions, and suggestions are provided to help you think about what you want and need to do. The guide can be used as a whole or as a quick reference for a specific topic. You may refer to the contents page for information about the details you need, or you can simply go to the section at the end of each chapter that addresses the immediate questions that you need to answer.

This guide is nondenominational and can be used when planning either a religious or a secular service. The information presented here is intended to help you think about the time before death and plan a funeral service for yourself or a loved one. If you are preplanning your funeral, you may speak with your family, minister, or funeral director and make some of the selections concerning the type of service desired, and music and readings you would like used. You may use the contents page to help you find those details you want to preplan. Funeral directors are prepared to help those who want to preplan the arrangements concerning the selection of burial plots and caskets or cremation urns to be used. This can be done before there is a need to enter a nursing home or hospital.

Since the services are carried out by the survivors, the voice of this guide is directed to those of us left to bury a loved one. However, you may use this guide to plan your own funeral if you want to. Facing the end of life, our own or that of a loved one, is not easy. The ideas and examples presented here offer a way for you to think about how to stay present to one another, as well as to the one who is dying, in the time before death and after the death occurs. We use ceremonies to mark the important events and changes in our lives. These rituals come out of ordinary experiences that shape us and influence who we are. Certainly, the time before and after a death occurs impacts the course our lives take. The use of ceremony and ritual offers us the opportunity to give form and expression to this experience.

There is not a right or wrong way to face death. Each of us comes to a place of acceptance in our own way and in our own time. This guide is intended to help you through a time of change. Be gentle with yourself and those around you. Make the most of these opportunities, for they come but once.

Each of us, at some time, will face the death of a loved one or our own death. Hospice provides support and care for patients and families facing end-of-life care needs. Hospice views dying as a normal process and does not hasten or postpone death but believes that care can be provided to make what ever time is left comfortable for patients and their families. Hospice is a program of support services of medical personnel, social workers, chaplains, clergy, and volunteers that provide care in the home or in a hospice facility. Hospice care may be provided by Medicare and most private insurance programs.

Death and dying raises many questions and issues that require our attention. The decisions we make about end-of-life care involve such issues as termination of treatment, quality of life, and how to make the time left comfortable for all involved with the care.

CHAPTER 1

There can be no more bitter time, nor
cherished time, than in the dying time. The
hours between darkness and light, fear and
love, despair and hope, linger in the dying
time. We wish for an end only of the
uncertainty. We seek peace that
passes all understanding . . .

IN THE DYING TIME

Living in the shadow of death is difficult. It requires a balancing act that most of us manage, not because anyone provides a recipe for success, but because we must. For the person dying, the process may be conscious or not. For those of us attending to the needs of the dying one, the process is an ebb and flow between knowledge and denial. We all adjust to our circumstances, making choices along the way, doing the best we can to cope with what is present in our lives.

When the illness is prolonged and death is anticipated, we adapt ourselves to the demands of the immediate present. Our resources are spent in attending to the needs of the one dying and the changes that are occurring for ourselves. The process of coming to terms with the idea of death can be a slow one.

The weeks or months before death occurs can be filled with moments of great despair and great joy, as there is a heightened sense of the precariousness of life. Even with the knowledge of an eventual death, life continues. Gradually the sense of the impending loss recedes as we adjust to the reality. It is a long introduction to the time before death.

For some, the time before death can be short, with little time to prepare. An accident or sudden illness brings us to a hospital or emergency room unprepared for the reality of loss. Sometimes we have only days or hours in the time of dying, as is the case with an illness that moves swiftly, a heart attack, a stroke, or an injury that requires life support. Yet even in these times there comes a realization, if only for a short time, that death will come. The dying time signals the shift from hope of recovery to the painful recognition that death will come instead. In the chaos each of us tries to think about what to do or say.

When the reality finally comes, and we can see or hear the change in our loved one's condition, every fiber in our being may cry out, "Not yet! I'm not ready! It's too soon!" We may want to run anywhere but straight into the arms of death. Painfully, the realization comes that we cannot change what will be, any more than we could stop the sunrise. There is before us two choices: to run, or to enter the stillness and to face that which we cannot change. Such sorrow, such pain. It is there in the running as much as in the stillness.

The dying time comes, against our will. In this time, we can see that the cycle of life is larger than we are. Birth and death, like the changing of the seasons, move by a force greater than you or me. How difficult it is to understand that we cannot control the outcome. We search to find a way to accept what is coming, even in the face of our denial and sorrow. We know death will signal the end of our loved one's physical presence among us.

Difficulties in the Time Before Death

There is a weariness that comes with living in the shadow of death. No matter what the illness is or the circumstances are, the time before death takes its toll on us— mentally, emotionally, spiritually, and financially. All of us, during this time, struggle to handle trying situations. We do our best to balance the impact of this time for ourselves and those around us. Often, we try to protect each other from our thoughts or feelings.

The task of staying present to one another in the time before death can be as stressful for the dying one as it is for those of us who will survive. Probably one of the most complex issues is how to speak what is in our minds and hearts when emotions and feelings are raw and painful. How do we prepare to say good-bye to one who means so much? How can we stay present when there is so much fear? Fear of the unknown, fear of the intensity of our feelings, fear of the atmosphere surrounding death, fear of failure of not being able to cope, fear of saying or doing the wrong thing. There are as many fears as there are people who have them.

Fear is a natural response to the unknown. It is a part of the range of human emotion. Fear, in and of itself, like any other emotion, is neither good nor bad. It just is. We try to act in spite of our fear. How we respond to our emotions, and how we handle difficult situations, are questions we all try to answer. Many people are afraid to be with someone when they die. What will happen? What will it be like? We fear for ourselves and for the one who is dying. It is an experience that is hard to anticipate, much like any major life change, full of both pain and comfort.

Most of us cannot bring ourselves to give voice to the questions or thoughts that are our constant companions during this time. Sometimes it is because we are not clear about what we can say, sometimes it is because we do not want to upset someone else. We think our feelings and thoughts will change or go away if we remain silent. We struggle with our regrets, with what has been unsaid.

We hesitate to speak openly about death for two reasons. First, we believe that if we do not give voice to our questions or thoughts, maybe they will not happen (or at least maybe we will not have to admit they are happening). Some call this denial, magical thinking, practical survival, or a foolish attempt at bravery. Second, when we do talk about the questions, we may not readily find the answers. For instance:

> How can I ever tell you what you have meant to me?
> What will death be like?
> Are you afraid to die?
> What will I do without you?

When we begin to give voice to the experience of the dying time, we open ourselves to the grief and sadness of the process. We struggle with all the other emotions present or triggered by the sorrow. We may feel too overwhelmed or believe we cannot cope with the intensity of our feelings or emotions. If we can remember that the intensity will pass and allow the grief to move through us instead of fighting so hard against it, we might cope a little easier. It will not take the grief away or stop the sorrow, but it will help increase our belief that we can survive or manage in this time.

For some of us, the time before death becomes especially challenging as we try to manage our emotions. We try to understand when to keep silent and allow others room for their thoughts or expressions. We learn to bear the unknown without overwhelming others with our needs, demands, fears, or anxious expressions of our questions and thoughts. It is a balancing act.

Balancing our needs and the needs of others is difficult for all involved. During this time, we must distinguish between the silence that comes from distancing ourselves from others when we are anxious and the silence that simply provides room for others to express themselves without interference from us. There are no easy answers, or right or wrong ways to handle ourselves. One can only make an effort to try to be as thoughtful and respectful to others, and to ourselves, in this time. Do not be afraid to talk to one another.

Using a Ritual Before Death

For some of us, the memories of events, experiences, or conversations with our beloved are recalled. In those moments we may sense the pattern or see the connections and glimpse the deeper reality that holds us together. It is a time of great sorrow and confusion. Rituals are an expression of our experiences. They elevate the ordinary event, giving it depth and richness. The reality of the time before death brings a change in ourselves and those around us. How do we stay present when someone is dying? What do we want to say before death comes?

Many people find it hard to manage during this time, feeling at a loss without a sense of direction. Some may be afraid of rituals. Some do not see the need for rituals or believe rituals do not matter. Others, however, find that the use of rituals or ceremonies before the death occurs provides a sense of peace amidst the sorrow. Rituals provide a gentle framework for marking the significant change in our lives.

A ritual in the dying time helps us to give voice to all that is in our hearts. It provides a place for us to express our thoughts and feelings. Rituals call us to pause and see the connections we have with one another and answer the need we have within to know we are not alone. Many religious traditions provide a framework for rituals in the time before death. Using ritual does not signal the end of hope but acts as a means for us to accept the reality we face. You may find that using certain rituals or ceremonies before death occurs provides a way to ease the chaos and give a sense of direction for all involved.

Prayers for the dying can be found in many traditions. The Catholic tradition has the Sacrament of Anointing, prayers said with and for the one who is dying. Protestant traditions have prayers recited with or for the person before death. The Jewish tradition contains the Vidui, a prayer that is said by or for the person who is dying. These prayers in the time before death give us a way to speak the unspeakable. The rituals serve to focus our minds, helping us to stay present to the one who is dying, as well as to one another during this time. Rituals quiet our fears and ease our pain temporarily.

> A man sat with his mother as she lay dying in the hospital. In the stillness of the night, he sang to her the Bohemian hymns that she had taught him as a child. In recognition of the pain of his loss and the acknowledgment of her life, he found meaning from an experience of long ago. In the sound of his voice, in the music of their bond, he spoke of their connection. She died later that day.

Did he know she would die that day? It's possible. What is important is that he found a way to talk with her before she died. Singing, reading poetry, wiping a fevered brow are all rituals in the time before death, for the dying itself elevates our experience. It is when we make the conscious effort to stay present to one another, that rituals occur spontaneously. Sometimes the dying time is brief. To gather to pray, sing, or read poetry in the presence of the dying one helps give us a way to attend to the one who is dying.

For one family gathering again was important to balance the stress of waiting against the fear of loss.

> A family gathered at the hospital, the last family member arriving a short time before the death. They gathered around the bed where their father lay in a coma and recited prayers from their background.

We take a break from the care, the management, the weight and the struggle of it. We pause to allow room for the whole of life to enter, not only the pain and sorrow. We gather, not so much to rehash what has happened or ignite old conflicts, but to acknowledge that life is full of both joy and sorrow.

> Another family cared for their grandmother at home. They gathered around her bed as she lay in a coma, unable to respond. They began by reciting prayers they had grown up with, and then each in turn said what they were most grateful for and what they would remember about her. Tears filled their eyes, and many voices broke with emotion. When they finished, they took turns once again, sitting with her and keeping watch.

Some people find that staying present to the dying person asks us to listen to the deeper questions: Who am I? Why am I here? What are my beliefs? It is an opportunity to pause and enter the spiritual in which we all live, but the awareness of which is dimmed by the routine of life.

Rituals in the dying time give us the opportunity to embrace life, even as death approaches. We try to acknowledge all we have been, done, and seen. Life, in all its glory, all its pain and sorrow, all its ups and downs, is recognized.

> A young man and his family were taking turns sitting with their aunt and sister. The death, which at first appeared to be days away, lingered over a

period of three months. For the young man, the hours spent at her bedside were long and filled with anguish. He began to use prayer and song as a nightly meditation both for himself and his aunt.

In our ceremony we begin to still our fears, quiet our anger, and soothe our anxiety. We begin to touch and express the tremendous sadness that runs underneath it all, the pulse of the dying time. Rituals provide a gentle means of staying present before death. We gather to pray and bless our loved ones, helping to release them from this life. They take a journey on which we cannot go. We release our hold on them, both for ourselves and for them.

Planning a Ritual Before Death

The comfort of a familiar ritual can give the structure needed at a time when it is difficult to create one on our own. Many of us are unaware of the simple format of prayers and blessings provided by our religious traditions. Talk with a chaplain or your spiritual leader to help you understand and use the rituals provided by your faith tradition. They are there to provide comfort in the time before death. You can also create a simple ceremony from your experiences.

As you think about the ceremony, feel free to draw from your history, your life. Determine how you want to put it together. Regardless of one's ethnicity, religion, or sex, we all have a history of the ways in which we gather. Look to the richness of your life to see what you want to do. The ritual can be planned by or with the dying person. It may be that we will need to talk with one another about what we may want to do. The ceremony can be a reflection of what we have been and where we are going.

We begin by inviting those who are important to us to gather in community and to celebrate life. We find the symbols that are an outward expression of what we value—books that have added a richness, music we have enjoyed, photos of the people and places in our lives, flowers we have treasured, hobbies we have a passion for, and gifts we have received. These mementos are but a small representation of what gives meaning to our lives. We may look to our own religious background to find a ritual or ceremony to use during the time before death.

Ask for assistance from someone close to you—a friend, family member, a chaplain, or spiritual leader in your faith tradition. Most people will respond, willing to help if possible. The ceremony can be simple, with a favorite reading or thoughts you wish to share, a collection of meaningful experiences, or a symbolic reflection of your life. It can be a familiar form like a liturgy or a gathering of friends to sing and listen. It can be as varied as there are people; we seek only to open ourselves to an experience that brings us closer to one another. If we allow ourselves to embrace the time before death, the unexpected can occur.

The ceremony will not change who we have been, but offers instead a chance to be open to change. It will not take away our pain and sadness, nor the anger and anguish, but offers instead an easing of the intensity of our emotions. Gather to be open to the presence of love, entering the sacred time for just a moment. Life, in all its difficulties, presents moments of joy amid sorrow. We can be open to the transformation of this time.

Choose the place if you can. If you are limited physically because of a nursing home, hospital, or hospice, bring with you the mementos that hold meaning and gather together. Eat if you can, laugh and cry. It is simply to be open to the grace present when we join our hearts, open to all that is, all that can be. Do not be afraid to say good-bye. We may have the opportunity to have a planned ritual or may instead use a simple prayer. Rituals can offer a way for reconciliation, for giving voice to what may be difficult to say. Make use of this time in whatever way is meaningful for you.

Prayers for the Time Before Death

PRAYER FOR A PEACEFUL DEATH

—*Illuminata: Thoughts, Prayers, Rites of Passage,* Marianne Williamson

Dear God, I think that I am going to die. I think that I'm going to leave this world. Give me strength, Lord, that I might not fear. I know God, that when I leave I do not die, that when I die I shall continue to live in Your arms, in Your mind, in Your spirit forever.

And yet, dear Lord, my heart beats wildly. I am so scared. My heart breaks, to be leaving those I love: my friends, my mate, my children, my loves. And yet I know I shall not be leaving. Heal my heart that I might know this. Heal theirs also that they might know that we are bound together forever, through Your power, which is greater than the power of death.

For the arms of God are the arms of life. Dear God, I surrender my body to You. If it serves Your purposes, than may I live, and if the arc of destiny now calls me home, then let me die in peace, dear God.

Send the Angel of Death to me when it is my time. Let me feel the Angel's tenderness as I exit this world and enter the next. Let me go from dark to light. Let me feel the love of God.

Please comfort me and those I love.

Now while I wait, now while I face my fears and my pain, let me see the truth and know Your peace. May my family and friends now feel the same.

For we shall not be torn asunder. Our love is larger that death. Our bond is eternal. Your life is with us always. So I believe, so shall I feel, now and forever.

Hallelujah, Lord.

For Yours is the power and the glory and love. You are with me as I am with You. Thank you, God, for what has been. Thank you, God, for what shall be.

Forgive me my darkness. Reveal to me Your light. Bless my family. Take care of them, my darling ones.

Take me Home. I willingly surrender. I shall not fear, for You are with me. Thank you, Lord.

Thank You, Lord.

Amen

or

Almighty God, Look on _____, whom you made your child in Baptism, and comfort him/her with the promise of life with all your saints in your eternal kingdom, the promise made sure by the death and resurrection of your Son, Jesus Christ our Lord.

or

[Name], our brother/sister in the faith, we entrust you to God who created you. May you return to the one who formed us out of the dust of the earth. Surrounded by the angels and triumphant saints, may Christ come to meet you as you go forth from this life.

or

Christ, the Lord of glory, who was crucified for you, bring you freedom and peace.

Christ, the High Priest, who has forgiven all your sins, keep you among his people.

Christ, the Son of God who died for you, show you the glory of his eternal kingdom.

Christ, the Good Shepherd, enfold you with his tender care. May you see your redeemer face to face and enjoy the sight of God forever.

One young woman, with the assistance of her rabbi, worked with the traditional Vidui and "rewrote" the prayer together until it became the prayer of her death.

KAYLA'S PRAYER
—*Jewish Insights On Death and Mourning,* Jack Riemer

Listen to my voice, O Lord our God and God of my ancestors.

I lie here on the brink of life, seeking peace, seeking comfort, seeking You.

To You, O Lord, I call and to You, O Lord, I make my supplication.

Do not ignore my plea. Let Your mercy flow over me like the waters, let the record of my life be a bond between us, listen to my voice when I call, be gracious to me and answer me.

I have tried, O Lord, to help You complete creation, I have carried Your yoke my whole life. I have tried to do my best. Count my effort for the good of my soul, forgive me for when I have stumbled on Your path. I can do no more, let my family carry on after me, let others carry on after me.

Protector of the helpless, healer of the brokenhearted, protect my
beloved family with whose soul my own is bound. Their hearts depended
on mine. Heal their hearts when they come to depend on You.

Let my soul rest forever under the wings of Your presence, grant me a
share in the world-to-come. I have tried to love You with all my heart and
with all my soul, and even though You come to take my soul, even though
I do not know why You come, even though I am angry at the way You take
me, For Your sake I will still proclaim:

Hear, O Israel, the Lord is our God, the Lord alone.

The Lord is with me, I shall not fear."

The revised Scottish Episcopal funeral rite of 1987 includes the two following prayers:

Forgiving God,
In the face of death we discover
how many things are still undone,
how much might have been done otherwise.
Redeem our failure.
Bind up the wounds of past mistakes.
Transform our guilt to active love,
and by your forgiveness make us whole.
Lord in your mercy
Hear our prayer.

or

God our Redeemer,
you love all that you have made,

you are merciful beyond our deserving.
Pardon your servant's sins,
acknowledged or unperceived.
Help us also to forgive as we pray to be forgiven,
through him who on the cross
asked forgiveness for those who wounded him.
Lord, in your mercy
Hear our prayer.

Children and the Time Before Death

Children need and desire to be included. Death is not yet fearful for them. To be involved in the process of our struggle in the dying time will help them accept the finality of death. As we become more open and accepting, we make the way a little easier for the young ones, who will surely feel the loss for themselves as they watch our sorrow and grief. The more we remain open and approachable, the greater the gift for the children. They, too, have things to say and share. They, too, wish to have a voice. It is both our duty and our privilege to help them find and give expression to that voice.

Children are more aware than we give them credit. Their simple statements often address that which we, as adults, find more difficult to speak. They are the representation of our future and our hope, the visible reality of the hope we place in life for ourselves. They are indeed welcome.

Children can participate by reading a passage, creating a gift, writing, or drawing to express their feelings. Care should be taken to look out for them and to have an adult available who can answer any questions they might have or listen to what they might say. Young children may need to come and go during this time. Older children, if asked, would tell you they want to be included.

The best we can do for children is to be open to them. They can manage to cope with the tears or upset of those around them when we stay direct and available. They can see the expression of sadness and see that the adults are able to take care of themselves. For the children, it is what is unspoken that they are unsure about. That uncertainty can cause them difficulties. We can give them the opportunity to grieve along with us. Include them as much as possible as you plan the services you will use. Given the opportunity, children have much to offer us. Death is a great disruption. Allowing their participation in appropriate ways helps them to be grounded and provides a source of stability for them.

Questions to Consider

The time before death is a time of waiting. The use of ritual can help us bridge the gap between what we know and what remains unknown. You may discuss these questions with the one who is dying or as an aid to help you organize your thoughts. Rituals used in the time before death are simply a means to help us create a time where we consciously accept what we cannot change.

Prayers or rituals may be used more than once in the time before death. These are some of the many ways that we can try to stay present to one another in difficult circumstances. Every suggestion or question does not have to be used.

Do you want to use a ceremony or ritual before the death occurs?

_____

Where will you hold your service?

_____

Address:

_____

With whom do you wish to gather?

_____

_____

_____

How much time do you need?

_____

What will you bring?

_____

_____

Whom do you want to help you?

_____

What reading(s) have you selected?

_____

_____

Do you wish to contribute to the prayers recited?

_____

CHAPTER 2

The reaction to death is as varied as there
are human responses. All are normal,
all come automatically from
deep within ourselves . . .

WHEN DEATH OCCURS

No one can be sure of the exact moment of death. Sometimes as much as we might want to be with someone when they die it does not happen. Be gentle with yourself during this difficult time. There are many, many occurrences outside of our control.

How death occurs does not matter. Whether by accident, illness, suicide, or the natural course of the life cycle, we are shaken by its impact. Time is suspended for a moment. Memories flash through a mind that struggles to comprehend the void. The impact of death is universal. The loss is felt on every level because life as we know it has been altered. It is forever changed.

The tremendous emotional impact is felt and expressed in our first reaction. We hear the news and respond. Often we say, "No! I'm so sorry." In those quiet words, our grief is reflected. When death comes, the impact is powerful. We do not easily forget those moments. Tears may flow freely for some. Others stand stoically against a pain that comes unbidden. Some of us talk a lot, while others look for something to do. The reaction to death is as varied as there are human responses.

All are normal. All come automatically, from deep within ourselves. There is not a right or a wrong way to react to death. There is simply our reaction.

Spending Time with the Person Who Has Died

Sometimes the death is unexpected, shattering the normal course of life. Sometimes death comes gently, the natural completion of the life cycle. Open yourself to the experience. Stay with the body as long as you need to—touching, talking to your loved one, using the time to begin to say good-bye. Nursing homes and hospitals are prepared to allow you the time you need to stay with the body. You need to tell those around you that you want to stay with the body for a time.

If you happen to be with someone at the moment they die, some of the events immediately following death can be unsettling. All bodily functions stop. You will probably notice an odor. Death has a smell all its own. All human beings emit a similar odor at death. There may be an expulsion of bodily fluids because the muscles relax and there is no more bodily control. This can be unsettling and confusing because it is outside our normal realm of experience.

Death affects all of our senses and emotions, helping us immediately to begin to adjust to the changes it brings. The first reactions of shock and grief are soon overshadowed by the physical realities of death. The body of the deceased goes through some rapid changes. The body begins to cool, and the skin loses its color. For those of us present, our reactions vary from quiet acceptance of a natural end to shock, horror, repulsion, and confusion—sometimes even to denial that death has occurred.

It is difficult to imagine that the one we have loved is gone. On many levels we rage against the loss, hoping against hope that they will return. Breath comes no more.

Gradually, we have to accept that death has come instead. The physical changes that take place in the body of the deceased help us to assimilate the unchangeable.

Here are two examples of people's responses to the death of a family member:

> A family sits in the emergency room. The mother is holding the body of her young daughter who had accidentally drowned. She holds her, rocking back and forth, repeating her sorrow, finding it difficult to let go, in shock.

To be in the presence of such raw grief is difficult. We can hardly stand it. Hospital personnel have learned to respect this grief and will allow you some time to stay with the body after death comes.

> A daughter reaches the nursing home shortly before her mother dies. She calls family members, some of who make it there before, some after the death occurred. The family gathers in her mother's room, present with the body for some time, telling stories, remembering their time together.

Some deaths come easy. Some are hard to bear. Whatever you do, say, or feel is just the natural outpouring of your grief. Honor this time. It is part of the process, part of an experience with death. If you are participating in an organ donor program, you may not have a great deal of time to spend with the body. There are time constraints that must be followed when the organs are to be donated. If you or your family and significant others wish to remain with the body after death occurs, please inform the attending personnel to help you set up the privacy you need. This may be as simple as drawing a curtain to separate one part of the room from another or moving the body to a private room. You may request that a member of the pastoral care team come and assist you with the prayers or ritual you would like to use in the presence of the body. Many people have been surprised by the comfort they received when they stayed with the body after a death. It becomes a natural occurrence in an extraordinary experience. Take care to answer the questions of children if they are present.

Many of the prayers for the deceased, in the presence of the body, are not complicated. It is a simple act of prayer and releasing or commending the spirit to God or Higher Power. Many recite the Psalms or the Lord's Prayer or sing a hymn that has great meaning for them. Some people rely on their traditions at this time, using the prayers of their faith.

Examples of Prayers Used in the Presence of the Body

The Jewish tradition has a *Hevra Kadisha*, a traditional Jewish burial group or holy society. They are members of the community who have volunteered to take care of the preparation of the dead for burial. They offer *shmirah*, members who volunteer to stay on duty watching over the body of the dead until the funeral while reciting psalms or studying sacred literature. They offer *taharah*, the ritual purification and washing and dressing of the met (the dead), done with great reverence and respect for the one who has died. These acts of kindness are given freely as a sacred task willingly done, gratefully received.

The Christian tradition has prayers used after death, that are recited in the presence of the body, for the deceased and the family members. Here are some examples:

PRAYER FOR FAMILY AND FRIENDS
—*Pastoral Care of the Sick: Rites of Anointing and Viaticum,* Catholic Book Publishing Co.

God of all consolation,
in your unending love and mercy for us
you turn darkness of death
into the dawn of new life.
Show compassion to your people in their sorrow.

Be our refuge and our strength
to lift us from the darkness of this grief
to the peace of your presence.

Your Son, our Lord Jesus Christ,
by dying for us, conquered death
and by rising again, restored life.

May we then go forward eagerly to meet him,
and after our lives on earth
be reunited with our brothers and sisters
where every tear will be wiped away.

We ask this through Christ our Lord.
Amen

Into your hands, O merciful Savior, we commend your servant, [name].
Acknowledge, we humbly beseech you, a sheep of your own fold, a lamb
of your own flock, a sinner of your own redeeming. Receive him/her into
the arms of your mercy, into the blessed rest of everlasting peace, and
into the glorious company of the saints in light.

or

O Lord, support us all the day long of this troubled life, until the shadows lengthen and the evening comes and the busy world is hushed, the fever of life is over, and our work is done. Then, Lord, in your mercy, grant us a safe lodging, and a holy rest, and peace at the last; through Jesus Christ our Lord.

or

Dear God, heavenly Father, our hearts are full of sorrow at the death of our beloved. Help us in our grief to remember that life does not end with death. Help us to find comfort in your promise of life everlasting. Lord, we may not always understand your ways but we ask for your help to accept our loss and to trust in you that all things are in your keeping. Welcome our beloved home and send us comfort to be with us now. Amen.—J.M.

Some people find the prayers take the form of spontaneous action that seems to express the range of emotions present at the time of death. One mother writes of this time:

My son died at home, giving us the great gift of staying with his body for as long as we needed. We were able to bathe him and change him, allowing us time to perform those last and final acts of love and tenderness. The feel of death, its coldness and color, faded as we spent those precious moments with him. As we washed his body, we spoke of our thoughts—talking about him, to him, in some ways with him—speaking gently through the tears, easing our sadness.

Her experience is consistent with the experience of most people in years past when the preparation of the body occurred at home (as did the wake or memorial service). Birth and death were a part of everyone's experience, close up in our homes and communities. As we have been removed from touching death, the act of preparing the body has become harder to complete or even imagine. But it is simply taking care of your own. If you are comfortable or willing, the benefit is great. It helps to integrate the reality of death through the senses of sight and touch.

A simple blessing may be used, a gesture such as making the sign of the cross on the forehead of the deceased or holding the body of your loved one as the final song is sung. This simple ritual can be lead by a family member or friend. It is an honor and a comfort to stay present and release the spirit of a loved one. Children may benefit from this opportunity with the gentle guidance of adults. When you have completed your time with the deceased it will be necessary to address some of the immediate details that arise after the death occurs.

Organ and Tissue Donation, Autopsy

Organ and tissue donation is a program where the useful organs or tissue of the deceased are given to a living human being. They replace a heart, eyes, liver, or other body parts that are no longer working for the living person. Many people find that participating in this program allows them to have a sense that the life of their loved one has brought added value or meaning to the life of another. That, even in death, there is an opportunity to give life. Out of one person's tragedy comes a gift that gives some meaning to the survivors and certainly gives life and meaning to the recipients.

In most states, hospital personnel are now required by law to talk with you about the option of organ and tissue donation. The decision to participate in a donor program may or may not have been made before death. In many instances, a form has been signed by the deceased before death, stating a desire to participate in the donor program. If not, a form will need to be signed indicating that at least one family member has been contacted about this matter. Many people react with resentment or confusion to this process, viewing it as an intrusion on their grief. However, it is a practical matter that you may need to address. For some, this final act of giving life is comforting.

If you choose to donate, please inform the nurse or doctor and she or he will guide you through the rest of the process. It should be noted that some religions have conflicting views about organ and tissue donation. Your time to stay with the body of your loved may be limited if there is to be an organ or tissue donation.

Autopsy is another difficult procedure for some people to understand. The attending physician will determine if an autopsy is required. The family may request that an autopsy be completed. An autopsy sometimes helps family members by answering questions about the cause of death, especially when it was not expected. In some circumstances, autopsies must be performed for legal reasons when death is totally unexpected and the cause unknown. Any questions you have about whether an autopsy should be done or not should be asked. You may direct your questions to the physician or other medical personnel with whom you are in contact. Events move rapidly after the death occurs. For those of us left behind, the pain and sadness are crowded by the demands of moving forward into preparing for a funeral.

Contacting Family and Friends

It is an automatic response to want to contact those close to us to tell them that our loved one has died. We reach out to one another in our grief, receiving comfort and support during this time of sorrow. Immediate family members or close friends come to our side and help us with the task of telling others. Designate a friend to help with the calling. It is helpful to make a list of the names of the people that need to be contacted. The list should also include the phone numbers of those to be called. The person in charge of the calling can inform those on the list of the death and let them know that they can check the newspaper obituary for the specifics of the arrangements.

This simple message allows the calls to be made without the burden of gathering the specifics before making the calls. You may also ask some of the people you call to help you contact some of the people on the list. This eases the burden on one individual and allows others to help. Most people are more than willing to help with this task. You only need to ask. The process of planning the funeral requires a tremendous attention to detail.

Initial Arrangements

No matter where or how the death occurs, you will be asked which funeral home you will be using. This is because the body must be transported to the funeral home for preparations for the services. You will also be asked which place of worship you will want contacted. Often it is the funeral director who makes the contact with the place of worship to begin the initial arrangements.

If you have decided that you want to use the funeral rituals of your religious tradition it is extremely important that you contact the place of worship as soon as possible. The primary benefit for doing this is that you may begin to immediately access the help provided by those you contact and to take full advantage of all that your tradition has to offer.

Selecting a funeral home to coordinate the funeral service and burial can be as simple as relying on the place your family has used in the past or choosing one in your community. If you prefer cremation, funeral homes are able to help you with this or you can contact a cremation society. Hospital or nursing home personnel can help you make the initial contact. These contacts can be made at the same time.

If the death occurs at home, an attending physician must call to report the death and contact the funeral home. In the case of an unexpected death at home, the police or coroner will make the contact. If you know the name and number of the funeral home you are using, give the police or coroner that information. If you do not have a preselected funeral home or cremation society, use the yellow pages in the local phone book; look under the heading "Funeral." Ask family or friends for recommendations.

Questions to Consider

If you are with someone when they die, do you want to spend time with the body?

_____

Is there a favorite prayer or simple gesture you want to use?

_____

_____

Do you need or want a spiritual leader contacted to assist you?

_____

Do you wish to participate in the organ donor program?

_____

Who will help contact/notify others of the death?

	Designated Caller	**Phone Number**

Primary:

_____

Alternate:

_____

Hospital and nursing home staff are familiar with helping you make the contact after the death has occurred.

Contacting the Funeral Home, Church, or Cremation Society

Name of funeral home or cremation society:

_____

Address:

_____

Phone number:

_____

Contact person:

_____

Name of church:

_____

Address:

_____

Phone number of church:

_____

Contact person:

_____

Cremation services are also listed under the heading "Funeral" in the yellow pages.

CHAPTER 3

In this time we seek clarity of thought and a
brave heart. In a time of great disruption
we search, seeking answers for
what must be done . . .

DECISIONS TO BE MADE

Death can come unexpectedly, or as a welcome relief to prolonged suffering. However, the loss is the same for us all—irreversible and permanent. Embracing life, celebrating all of its experiences, and attempting to communicate the essence of life are some of the purposes of funeral rites. For those of us left to attend to the details, the funeral becomes a pivotal event, marking the passage of a relationship and the change in ourselves.

When we plan the details of the service, we can fully embrace and experience the funeral as an expression of our grief. Though the process may be painful, a sense of completion comes out of the full expression of our experience. The lasting benefit is that forever after the funeral experience is a reference point for easing our pain, moving us forward into life again. We remember those life-changing moments that define us time and time again, drawing strength, meaning, and understanding from the insights gained.

If we draw our wisdom from the Torah, the Koran, the Bible, the teaching of Buddha, Confucius, or native religions, it is important to provide expressions of those beliefs. We use the words of poets and philosophers or our own words from within to give voice to who we are. We sing the ancient melodies, recite the verses that move us and sustain us, dance the sacred dance, beat the drums, or gather in silence and prayer. We listen to one another and draw strength from one another to move forward on our path without the bodily presence of our beloved. Make the most of this opportunity, for it comes your way only once. When planning the service, draw on the experiences of others. The death may be anticipated or unexpected. In both cases, the details of planning a funeral service remain the same.

The funeral director or leader of your religious tradition is available to help you through this process. It is important for you to be direct with them about what you want to include in the service(s). They are there to act as guides, but you are the one who is planning the service(s). When you meet with both the funeral director and the place of worship you will be asked about the type and place of the services. The information presented here is offered to help you answer those questions more easily.

Issues to Consider When Planning a Funeral

The time before death and after a death occurs is one of the most difficult experiences that we encounter. One of the first questions we struggle with is "What do we do now?" Funeral preparations require that we make many decisions very quickly. You will need to determine if you will hold a service within your religious tradition or if you will design a service yourself. You will also need to determine what the services will be and where they will be held.

This section will help you think about what type of service you want to hold as well as identify some issues related to the decision to use a religious tradition and those that specifically relate to designing the service yourself. Those concerns related to cremation and the different services that can be held are explored. A checklist of thoughts about the services and specific requests an individual may have about their funeral is provided at the end of the chapter. This can be completed before the death occurs if the time is available.

Using a Religious Tradition

It is important to remember that there may be scheduling conflicts with the place of worship. Some places of worship do not hold funeral services on Sundays or holy days, and there may be time conflicts with other services already scheduled. The funeral director can help with this issue. The contact person at the place of worship is well trained to help you through the days following a death. If you prefer, you can have the services held at the funeral home and performed or presided over by the clergy or the funeral director.

Many of us rely on our religious traditions to guide and sustain us in times of difficulties. In many ways, the structure of a tradition gives the comfort of familiarity in a time of great upheaval and disruption. The few days immediately after a loved one's death are intense and clouded due to the emotional rendering that happens. A familiar service gives us a safe harbor in which to express our sadness and grief. We become grounded in the repetition, finding some solace in the stability offered by the unchanging form.

Our religious traditions provide the framework for what we must do to plan a service for a loved one. We are not designing a service. Instead we use the traditional services of our faith to give comfort in our grief and expression of the meaning of our relationship with our loved one. You will work with your place of worship when you plan the service(s). It is important that you contact your place of worship as soon as possible to begin planning the services.

If you are burying a loved one who had an active faith, it is appropriate that the service(s) follow a religious framework even if you yourself do not hold those beliefs.

If you do not have a place of worship, perhaps your parent was active in a church, synagogue, or mosque; you should contact their place of worship and make use of the services provided for funeral rites. Most places of worship welcome people to make full use of the funeral and burial rituals offered. If you are not familiar with what is offered, you will need to take the time to ask what guidelines a religious tradition may have. Outlines for various religious traditions are provided in chapter 7 and the appendices.

Choosing Not to Use a Religious Framework

When you design the service yourself, you have made the decision not to use any traditional religious framework. You will need to determine if you will have the burial before the service or after the completion of the service. You will also need to select an individual to lead the service. For some people, designing the service themselves provides the opportunity to create a service that is a reflection of who their loved one was, what they meant to the survivors, and what they believe. Creating the service allows for the chance to give expression to the joy of knowing the loved one as well as the sorrow of their loss.

The funeral home is generally used as the place for the funeral services when a specific religious tradition is not used. However, some people may choose to have the service held at home or in another place. You will need to discuss the location of the service with the funeral director. An outline for designing the service yourself is provided in chapter 7, "Nontraditional Services."

Type of Burial

The decision about the type of burial used may affect the order of the services you choose to have. You will need to determine if you will use cremation or burial in a casket. Cemeteries or mausoleums are generally used to bury the remains. Some people want their cremated remains scattered instead of buried. Discussion about this issue appears in the following section.

Cremation

The decision to use cremation is usually a personal one, but some religious traditions have very strict policies regarding its use. Many faith traditions allow the use of cremation but require that the cremated remains be buried accompanied by the full burial rites provided by the religious ceremony. Some faith traditions strongly discourage the use of cremation, and others do not approve of the use of cremation. Some religious traditions allow the cremated remains to be present at the funeral service while others do not. If cremation is permitted, you will need to ask how the burial of the remains is to be completed. It is important that you understand your faith teaching about cremation and respect the guidelines they offer. Religious traditions reflect a great reverence for life and the human body. It is out of respect that the remains are buried.

Cremation of the remains can occur before or after the services. Sometimes a private burial for family and invited guests is held before the service. The memorial service is then held at the funeral home or place of worship with the community invited to attend. For some services the cremated remains are present at the service and the burial is completed after the service is ended. For others, the body is cremated after the funeral service has been held. In this case the casket is present at the funeral service and then the remains are cremated just before the burial.

Some people request that their remains be scattered at a specific location, or the survivors choose to scatter the cremated remains. Usually a short service, prayer, or gathering is held before releasing the remains. You may want to talk with the funeral director, spiritual leader, or family members or close friends as you sort through the issues concerning cremation. There may be differences in people's thoughts and feelings about this issue. Please remember to be gentle and tolerant of one another as you clarify your thoughts about this topic.

Types of Services

No matter the type of service—religious, traditional, nontraditional, or secular, whether held in a church, a funeral home or a synagogue, or other location—you will need to coordinate the service with the clergy, rabbi, priest, minister, spiritual leader, and/or funeral home director.

Funeral and burial customs can differ from one culture to the next. Generally the funeral services can include a visitation or vigil for the deceased or wake, the funeral or memorial service, and burial or graveside services. Some religious traditions offer all three types of services; some do not. A brief description of the different services are offered here to help you understand the differences between the services. You would discuss the particular structure of the service(s) with your place of worship or with the funeral director if you are putting together your service without the use of a religious framework.

Visitation, Wakes, Viewing, or Vigil for the Deceased

This is a time for the family and friends to come together and pay their respects to the one who has died. There is usually a short service included. This is a time for music, reflections, and prayer, if you choose. The duration of the service is usually from one to three hours. During this time people come when they can, expressing condolences to the family and paying their respects to the one who has died. This can be held the evening before the funeral service or a few hours before the funeral service itself. If held on the same day as the funeral, it usually begins a few hours or an hour before the service. The body may be present in the casket, and the casket may be open or closed.

Some cultures have longer periods of mourning before the services. More people are embracing their cultural heritage and traditions and want to include them in the services that will be held. Talk with your funeral director or place of worship about some of the specific traditions you want to use.

The wake or visitation gives those who may not be able to attend the funeral an opportunity to say good-bye to one who has been important to them. Many others outside the family are affected by the death of our loved one. The wake or visitation is an opportunity for them not only to express sympathy to the family and close friends, but to honor the end of a relationship that has had significance for them as well.

The time spent with others from the community, those people who were a part of the life of our loved one, helps us as much as it helps them. Friends, colleagues, and acquaintances will appreciate the time provided for them. The visitation or wake is more informal than a funeral or memorial service. It allows people to talk to one another, as well as with the family members. Many people want to speak with us, to remember their stories or to offer words of comfort.

This can be a particularly trying time for the family because it is struggling with private grief, at a time when they are asked to publicly acknowledge death. As much as we want to know our loved one's life mattered to others, it is sometimes difficult to acknowledge the grief of others in the midst of our own. The public display of emotion is difficult, but filled with many moments of healing for those who grieve. The vigil or wake gives us the opportunity to see the depth of this life and to acknowledge we are all part of the experience.

Funeral or Memorial Services

A funeral service has the body present at the service in either the casket or cremation urn. Some people choose to have a private burial before the service. A memorial service does not have the body present at the service. The structure of this service can be the same as that used for a funeral. The funeral or memorial service is a formal service, similar to the formality of a wedding, baptism, or bar/bat mitzvah. The purpose is to honor the one who has died and to comfort those who mourn. The service is clearly defined by its structure and purpose and helps us acknowledge the meaning of the life that has passed, as well as the death itself. A memorial service can be held if the death occurs out of state or the body is not present because of a natural disaster, accident, or other circumstance.

Location of the Services

Once you have made the decision about what services you will have and if you will be using a religious framework or not, you will need to determine where the services will be held. Religious services can be held at the place of worship or at the funeral home. Some people are choosing to hold the wake at home and the funeral service at the place of worship. You will need to discuss your decision with the funeral director and place of worship if necessary.

Burial or Graveside Services

The burial or graveside services can occur before or after the visitation, funeral, or memorial services. The burial service can be private, by invitation only, or may be open to all those who come to the service(s). Burial services are generally short and consecrate the ground where the deceased will be buried. This service is usually conducted by the spiritual leader, minister, rabbi, priest, or deacon from the place of worship. It can also be lead by a family member or designated individual if you are not using a faith tradition.

Questions to Consider

The following questions are provided to help you think about what arrangements will be made. You may discuss these with the one who is dying or as an aid to help you organize your thoughts.

Will you use a religious tradition for the services?

_____

Will cremation be used? If so, before or after the services?

_____

Will you have a visitation, wake, viewing, or vigil for the deceased?

_____

Where will it be held?

_____

Address:

_____

Date and time:

_____

Will the burial occur before or after the services?

_____

Will you have a funeral service or a memorial service?

_____

Where will the funeral or memorial service be held?

_____

Address:

_____

These questions will be asked or addressed again when you meet with the funeral director and/or place of worship.

The following information is provided to help you gather basic information about the arrangements that are to be made. This information may be provided by the deceased before death or you may use these statements as a way to think about the type and manner the deceased may have wanted the services to be conducted.

Personal Thoughts about the Services

The following ideas were adapted from *Jewish Insights on Death and Mourning*.

Name:

_____

List immediate living relatives:

_____

Funeral Arrangements

I would like the services to be held at:

_____

I want the following services held: (check if selected)

_____ wake

_____ vigil

_____ visitation

_____ I do not want an open casket.

_____ funeral service

_____ memorial service

_____ I prefer my family select an appropriate casket or cremation urn.

_____ I prefer to be buried in a simple casket or simple cremation urn.

_____ I do not want to be embalmed unless necessary.

I would like the following music and readings (include poetry or verse if desired) used at my wake, visitation, or vigil:

_____

_____

_____

I want to be dressed in: (please specify)

_____

_____

I would like the following type of burial:

_____ I do not want to be cremated.

_____ I would like to be cremated.

_____ traditional burial/cemetery name:

_____ I want the family to remain until the conclusion of the interment (lowering) service.

I would like my ashes scattered at the following place:

_____

_____

I would like the following readings and music to be included in my funeral service:

_____

_____

_____

I would like the music performed by:

_____

_____

_____

I would like the following people to act as pallbearers:

_____

_____

_____

_____

I would like the following people to speak at my service:

_____

_____

_____

_____

Please mention the following about me:

I was active in:

_____

_____

_____

I have the following hobbies and interests:

_____

_____

_____

I would like these aspects of my personality remembered:

_____

_____

_____

*Gathering strength we begin to attend to the
details of accepting the death of our loved
one. We seek clarity of thought and
a gentle hand to guide us . . .*

AT THE FUNERAL HOME

It is very helpful to bring along family members or friends to help you through the decisions you will be making. Taking a family member or close friend along to the funeral home helps ease the stress of feeling alone or overwhelmed with the details. They help us think a little more clearly about what we want to do. It is comforting to talk with someone who understands our feelings and emotions. Ask for help when you need it. While most people do not know exactly what you need, they stand ready to help you if called upon. There are so many choices that the grief can cloud your thinking. Emotions are intense and even thinking about making a decision is difficult.

For some, going to the funeral home is too much to bear. This is perfectly normal. Generally, someone among family or friends is able and willing to meet with the funeral home to begin making the arrangements. For instance:

> An elderly man died after a long illness, leaving his wife and five grown
> children to attend to the details of his funeral. The wife refused to go to

the funeral home. The family selected one of the sons to make the arrangements. He was accompanied by a brother-in-law who had buried his father years earlier. The two men, in frequent contact with the other family members, made the initial arrangements at the funeral home.

It is important to remember and to respect that each one of us has different limits. Each one of us also has different interests and talents that are invaluable when making funeral arrangements. Funerals tend to bring out both the best and the worst in us. Both our strengths and weaknesses contribute to the experience of planning a funeral. If we recognize that everyone has something to give, as well as the limits that are present in all of us, the time ahead may be a bit more manageable. We handle what we can, the best that we can.

When you meet with the funeral director, you will need to make a number of decisions. The funeral director is trained to help you plan for traditional services, cremation, and burial. He or she will help to coordinate the services you will be using. If you will be holding the service at a place of worship, you will need to give the funeral director the name of the place of worship you are using.

Here is a brief list of what issues or tasks you will need to address at the funeral home or cremation society:

- cost of services provided
- transportation of the body from place of death
- type of burial (casket or cremation), selection of casket or cremation urn
- place of burial, selection of burial plot if needed
- open or closed casket
- selection of clothing used for burial
- embalming if necessary or required, preparation of the body

- selection of type of service to be used
- choosing the time and place of the services
- obituary notice
- memorial cards/funeral programs or bulletins
- guest book

Questions are provided at the end of this chapter to help you with decisions that must be made.

Cost of Services Provided

The funeral director is required by law to review the cost of the funeral and to provide you with the details of his or her services. When your feelings of shock and sadness are still fresh, it is especially difficult to focus on the cost details. Having someone close for support and help makes this process easier.

Transportation of the Body

The funeral home will make arrangements to move the body from the place of death to the funeral home. They will also move the body from the funeral home to the place where the funeral services will be held, and to the final burial place.

Place of Burial, Selection of Burial Plot

During your meeting, you will be asked which cemetery you will use if the body will be buried. You will need a cemetery plot to bury the body. Some people will have purchased a cemetery plot before the death occurred. Some people who select cremation choose to scatter the ashes or the deceased has requested the remains be scattered in a specific place or manner.

If a cemetery has not been selected in advance, you will need to choose a place for the burial. Some people have a family cemetery that will be used. The funeral director will help you make the necessary arrangements with the cemetery. If necessary, he or she will help you contact a local cemetery or you can contact the cemetery yourself.

Selection of Casket or Cremation Urn

Many people today have preselected a casket or urn. If preplanning has been done, the choice of a casket or urn may already have been made. For those of you who are making the decision now, the funeral director will provide the information needed to help you make this decision.

An urn is used when the body will be cremated. If you are selecting the casket or urn after the death has occurred, it is important to remember that your selections are not a measure of your love for the deceased. Selecting the casket or urn is difficult for most of us. It is a visual symbol of the death. Some people choose not to look at the selections but make a choice based on the cost and description. This is entirely appropriate if it is your decision.

For most people, cost is a real concern because life insurance coverage may not be available to help pay for the funeral. If you prefer, ask to see the selection of available caskets before deciding. Your choice must be comfortable for you, both emotionally and financially. The funeral director will go over the cost of each selection. They will also let you know whether there is a need for a grave liner and/or a vault.

Embalming

The funeral director may discuss embalming, a method used to preserve the body before burial, with you. This procedure may be required in situations where there is a time delay in burying the body. Some states require this procedure. You may ask if it is necessary for the type of burial you will be using. Some faith traditions do not use embalming unless needed.

If the casket will be open during the vigil, the body will be embalmed in preparation for the service. It is most helpful to bring a picture of the deceased to the funeral home so the professional can ensure the deceased will look as he or she did when alive. Obviously, death affects the way a person looks, so it is very helpful to bring a picture for the funeral director to use as a guide in the preparation.

Open or Closed Casket

You must decide if the casket will be open or closed during the service. The decision to have the casket open or closed is one for the family to make. There are reasons for either choice. Having the body present allows us to say farewell to the physical presence of our beloved. It gives us confirmation of death and helps to prepare us to face the future without them. Seeing the body in the stillness of death helps us know the reality of death and to accept that our loved one is gone.

Some of us resist having the casket open, fearing that the memories of seeing the body in the stillness of death will overpower the images we have of our loved one in life. The truth of the matter is that we will always remember them as they were when they were alive. The shock of death will fade, gently leaving us with the images of life.

Others resist viewing the body and fear that the grief, sorrow, or shock will be too overwhelming with which to cope. There is no getting around it: Death is painful and coping with the loss of someone close to us is difficult, but with time we will incorporate the loss and adjust to the change. The ache itself is neither good nor bad. It is simply a natural response to our loss. We cope because we have to and because we can. An open casket allows family and friends to face the reality of death. As difficult as this is, it is necessary to help us cope, to comprehend with our minds as well as our hearts that our loved one has died. We know and believe because we have seen.

For those of us who must bury a loved one who has become unrecognizable, the grief is sometimes harder to manage. Often we wonder if it is really true that our loved one has died. We question whether a mistake has been made. In our hearts, we hold onto the hope that they might return. It takes time to accept that death has removed them from our lives.

In the case of an accident, a suicide, or when the dying time was especially painful, you may decide to have the casket open during a private time for your family and close friends. This intimate time will allow you to grieve with those closest to you, to touch and see in reality and to begin letting go.

> The mother of a young girl who drowned needed to see the body in the casket to realize her daughter was gone. The essence of her child was no longer held in the body. They had a private time for the family with the casket open before the community came, and the casket was closed during the time the community was present.

Selection of Clothing and Preparation of the Body

Another detail of a burial is the selection of clothing for the deceased. During the initial visit with the funeral director, it is appropriate to discuss what type of clothing the deceased will be buried in. Many people choose clothing from the wardrobe of the deceased. Some may buy a new suit or dress. Others choose to bury their loved one in a military or sports uniform, or the uniform of an organization to which they belonged. If you wish, you may help to dress the body at the funeral home. Speak to the funeral director about participating in the dressing of the body. In the past, the dressing of the body was handled by the family. Today, the task is generally handled by the funeral director. Some funeral homes may have some restrictions concerning this matter. If this is something you want to do, ask. Most funeral directors are willing to accommodate your wishes.

Many people who have helped with the dressing of the body for a loved one have expressed they found a great deal of comfort from that act. These final acts of love and care seemed a natural completion of their loved one's death. Touching the body during this time and performing specific tasks may help to ease the initial shock of their loss.

In some religious traditions, the preparation of the body is done by members of a burial society or by the family. Islam tradition require that a body be washed according to their religious teaching. The washing of the body is done by family members under the direction of the funeral director. Jewish burial societies are established to care for the dead. Volunteers in the society help to wash and prepare the body according to their rituals. If they request, family members may participate in the washing of the body.

Preparation of the body and the act of preparing the body for the funeral, are difficult tasks to think about. However, it is traditional in many cultures for family members to prepare their own for burial. The purpose of the initial meeting is to address the immediate details of when and where the services will be held. You may return later to the funeral home with a picture of the deceased and the clothes for the deceased.

Obituary

You will need to provide the funeral home with the information necessary for the obituary. The funeral home can place the obituary and make all the necessary arrangements with the local newspaper. They can also place the obituary in newspapers in other cities for you if, for example, the deceased lived for a time in another city. While many people find it easiest to have the funeral home take care of this detail, you may contact the newspapers yourself. If you contact the newspapers yourself, they will need the name of the funeral home to verify that a death has occurred. The cost is the same no matter who places the notice.

An obituary is a notice of a person's death. It requires at the least the name, date of birth, and date of death of the deceased. Some people choose to use the obituary as a place to publicly acknowledge the personality and accomplishments of the deceased. Often words of love, admiration, and remembrance are used. A note of fond farewell can be used, including a photo for print. The cost of the obituary is determined by the length of the copy. You may make the obituary as brief or as lengthy as you wish.

You may also state a preference for memorials, usually gifts of money, rather than flowers. If you state a preference for memorials, the memorials can be directed to an organization as a lasting tribute to the deceased. Memorials can be sent to any organization that had meaning for the deceased or has meaning for the survivors. Examples include schools, churches, hospitals, research organizations, charities, and some activist groups. The memorial can also be used to fund a child's education or care of the survivors. Members of the community will respond to the notice by either sending flowers or by making a contribution in honor of the memory of the deceased or both. Finally, the obituary will list the time and place of the funeral service(s). The family, friends, and acquaintances of the deceased can arrange to attend the service(s).

Memorial Cards

The funeral director may ask you to select a memorial card and program to be used at the service. Generally, there is a book with selections to choose from. You can select the design for the front of the card from selections offered. Usually, the back of a memorial card includes the name of the deceased, the deceased's dates of birth and death, the date and place of the services and the place of burial. If you choose to design the card yourself, information about how to do so is provided in chapter 6.

The decision to personalize the memorial card is optional. Whatever you choose will be appropriate for you. However, you have time, even if it seems short, to create a memorial card and program. Take time to think about what you want.

Funeral Programs / Bulletins

You may put together a complete program of the funeral, including readings, meditations, service format, pallbearers, music, and final commendations for the body. Some places of worship may offer to assist you. This can be great resource for you.

Ask if this help is available. When you reprint material to be used in the program or bulletin, permission to reprint is generally acknowledged. This is a simple procedure. Most places of worship reprint songs and readings for their regular services. The church staff is generally able to secure permission to reprint these materials for you and help with the placement of the acknowledgment within the program.

The program may also contain a written eulogy or, if you are planning your service, a letter or note to those who will survive you. You may design an original cover for the program or copy the cover from the memorial card. Using a computer makes this task easier, and sometimes church staff members are willing to help construct and type the program. However, it is not too difficult to do this yourself. A print shop can easily make copies in time for the funeral.

Even though you have only two or three days to complete all the arrangements, working together with family and friends makes it possible to find readings, scripture verses, poems, or other writings that are meaningful for you. Locating appropriate and meaningful writings will help give focus to your efforts to create a meaningful service. The content of the program can be put together from the information in chapter 6.

Guest Book

Many funeral homes provide a guest book as part of the services they offer. If no guest book is provided, you may wish to purchase one for use at the service. A guest book, placed where people can sign their names, serves as a record of those who attend. In the days, weeks, months, and years following a funeral the guest book takes on great meaning for the survivors. The guest book gives the survivors an object to hold which confirms the reality that many relationships were affected by the death of a loved one. The guest book also gives members of the community an opportunity to communicate their presence at the services.

Questions to Consider

Has your loved one left any instructions concerning their thoughts and wishes about their funeral arrangements?

_____

_____

_____

Has the type of burial been preselected? If so, list the information here:

_____

_____

_____

What type of burial do you choose: casket or cremation urn?

_____

Where will the burial be completed: cemetery or mausoleum?

_____

Address:

_____

Is there a family monument already in place?

_____

Do you need or want a marker for the grave site?

_____

Type, Time, and Place of Services

Will you hold a visitation, funeral, or memorial service?

_____

Will the burial be private or open to those attending the service?

_____

Where and what time will the services be held?

_____

_____

_____

Preparations for Burial

If possible, do you want to participate in preparing the body? In what capacity?

_____

Will you have an open or closed casket during the visitation, wake, or memorial?

_____

What clothing will be used for the burial?

_____

_____

Who will bring the clothing to the funeral home and what time will they need it?

_____

Will embalming be used?

_____

Will the funeral home need a picture of the deceased? Who will bring it?

_____

_____

Information for the Obituary

Will you place an obituary in the newspaper? How many days will it appear?

_____

_____

Obituary cost is determined by the length and number of days printed.

Which newspaper(s), local or other, do you want place the notice?

_____

_____

Name(s) that will appear in obituary notice (can include nicknames if desired):

_____

Date of birth and date of death:

_____

The following are optional:

Age and birthplace:

_____

List of survivors (names and/or relationship to the deceased):

_____

_____

_____

_____

_____

_____

Some people include the name of each child and their spouse. If a child dies, the parents' and siblings' names are often included in the obituary. Significant others and close friends can also be listed. A short biographical account of the deceased's life is appropriate.

Professional history:

_____

_____

_____

_____

Organizations the deceased belonged to:

_____

_____

_____

Military service, if any:

_____

_____

Personal accomplishments:

_____

_____

_____

Personal notes, poetry, and/or expressions of farewell can be listed here:

_____

_____

_____

List the organization(s) to which you want memorials directed:

_____

_____

Finally, the obituary will list the time and place of the funeral and burial service(s). The family, friends, and acquaintances of the deceased can make arrangements to attend the service(s).

Memorial Cards and/or Funeral Programs

Have you selected the memorial card or will you design your own?

_____

Deadlines to get card to printer and to funeral director:

_____

If you are choosing a predesigned card provided by the funeral home, what information do you want on the card?

_____

_____

_____

_____

_____

_____

Do you want to have a funeral program? If so, what information do you want in it?

_____

_____

_____

_____

_____

Refer to chapter 6 for ideas and thoughts about designing your own memorial card and/or funeral program.

Guest Book

Often the funeral home can provide a guest book for you if you wish. If it is not provided by the funeral home, assign someone the task of selecting it for you.

Do you want a guest book? Who will set it out and make sure there are pens?

_____

Memorial Gifts Received at the Service

Some people bring checks or donation for the designated memorial request to the service. Is there a basket or place set up to receive these gifts?

Who will be in charge of taking these contributions home?

_____

CHAPTER 5

The service helps to ground us in the
present, reflecting on the past. It is
a time that speaks to our hearts, all
that we cannot say individually . . .

AT THE PLACE OF WORSHIP

Each religious tradition has a rich history of rituals that are used in funeral services. The services have a format and structure that is well defined by the order of prayers, readings, and blessings used. The outline varies little from one funeral to the next. What does vary, of course, are the personal touches each of us brings to the experience. Personalizing the service of an existing faith tradition is a way to add particular meaning to the services you have. It is within the familiar rituals we use that we bring our voices and hearts to find comfort in a time of great disruption and sorrow.

When you contact the place of worship, you will need to decide what type of services will be held, the date, and the time of the services. Generally the meeting takes place at the place of worship. If you are unable to meet with them at their place of work, ask if they would be able to come to your home. Some will offer this service.

During this meeting, you will be given information about the specific guidelines for services used in your faith tradition and the date and time that will be available for services. The leaders of your place of worship are trained to help you plan the services. They provide the basic framework you will need to create a service that will reflect the meaning of the relationship you have had with the deceased and serve to honor that person's memory.

Discussing the Services

You will need to determine what type(s) of services you will have, a visitation, wake, or vigil for the deceased. Ask how this service is structured and what parts of the service the family may be responsible for. You will need to decide if a funeral or memorial service will be held and place of the burial service. You should discuss the type of burial you will be using and the order of the services. You may want the leader of your faith tradition to assist you with the services at the funeral home instead of a place of worship. You may choose to hold the visitation at home.

You may be able to place the cloth that covers the casket, or the family and close friends may be able to process into the place of worship with the casket at the beginning of the service. Family members or friends may be able to serve as readers, greeters, ushers, or pallbearers. You will need to ask if it is appropriate to offer eulogies or remembrances, and at which service can these contributions be given and who may present these. Ask where the reception will be held if you are having one. Any question that you have is appropriate to ask.

Here is a list of topics for you to cover with your place of worship:

- type of service(s) to be used
- guidelines for the services used
- identification of ways you can personalize the services
- location of service(s)
- type of assistance available for planning the service

Your religious leader will most likely be speaking about the deceased during the service. He or she will talk with you about the deceased to gather information about them for the service. A list of questions and topics for you to cover with your religious leader is provided at the end of this chapter. Ideas for personalizing the services, and samples of eulogies are provided in chapter 6 to help you think about what you might want to do.

Readings

You will want to talk about the selection of readings to be used in the service. Ask if you may select them and how many are needed for the service. You may select the readings from the Bible, other sacred scriptures, or religious writings. Some places of worship allow mediations or blessing from your cultural heritage to be used along with the prayers and blessings of the religious traditions. Ask if these additions would be appropriate and in what service they can be used.

Prayers

It may be allowed to write prayers of petition, or gratitude. These can be written by and read by the family or close friends of the deceased if it is appropriate to do so. Usually three or four prayers are said and can include prayers for the deceased, the survivors, the community, thanksgiving for the caregivers, or for help or guidance for others who face a similar situation.

Music

You can select the music to be used in the service. Generally, you need an opening song, offetory, communion, and closing hymn. Use the hymnal provided by the church to help you make your selections. Your place of worship can help you with these selections if needed. Find out if your place of worship can help provide musicians for the service(s). The topic of music selection is addressed in chapter 6.

Location of the Services

The visitation, viewing, or vigil for the deceased can be held in the church, funeral home, or family home. This service can be used even when cremation has been selected. The cremation can occur before or after the service is held. Cremation can occur before the final ceremony. For example:

> One family was faced with the death of their son in a skiing accident. They made the decision to hold the vigil for the deceased at the family home. They set the time for the services and the time when family members and friends could come to be with the family. The funeral services were held the following day at the church. The next day the immediate family went to the funeral home for a private service before the cremation. The parents, grandparents, daughter, and close friend of the deceased stayed during the cremation. They prayed, staying present to the spirit of their son, brother, and friend. The burial was a private service.

Some choose to have the visitation at the church the evening before the service. Some have both services held at the funeral home or have a vigil just before the service.

Graveside Services

The burial of the body can occur before or after the service. The prayers and readings used in the graveside service are provided by the church. You can add personal touches if you wish. The service is short and blesses the final resting place of your loved one.

Private Burials

You may have a private burial service for family and close friends followed by a memorial service and reception with the community. You may choose to have a memorial service if the burial is held in another state. It can be a time for the community to gather when travel to the funeral is not possible for a number of people touched by the loss of their friend or family member.

If you are having a private burial that occurs after the funeral service, have the religious leader announce to those present at the funeral that the family prefers a private burial. Those close friends you wish to accompany you to the graveside can be notified before the funeral service. If everyone at the funeral is welcome at the graveside, the leader may simply announce the location of the burial site. Usually, there is a procession from the funeral site to the burial site.

Disposition of the Cremated Remains

You will need to talk with the leader of your place of worship to determine what is the proper way to handle the disposition of the cremated remains. Some faith traditions allow the scattering of the remains. Some do not. It is a matter for you to discuss with your place of worship.

Questions to Consider

Some of the questions about the time and place of the service is repeated from the chapter on contacting the funeral home. The funeral home works closely with the place of worship that you are using and will help to coordinate the arrangements.

Who is helping to coordinate the service? Phone number:

_____

_____

When will you meet with him/her?

_____

Will you have a visitation or vigil?

_____

Will you have a funeral service or a memorial service?

_____

Planning the Services

Here is a list of questions that need to be addressed at the place of worship. It is helpful to go through the outline or guideline of the services provided by the place of worship before making any decisions.

What time and date are available for the service?

_____

What are the fees for the use of the place of worship and the musicians provided by the parish?

_____

Will you have an open or closed casket at the service?

_____

What readings will be used?

_____

_____

_____

It is helpful to use a hymnal or a book of worship to select music for the services.

What music have you selected for the funeral/memorial service?

_____

_____

Eulogies and Personal Contributions

Give some notes on the deceased's life to the person who will be giving the sermon or eulogy during the service. Ask if you or someone else may give a eulogy. Also ask when the appropriate time for the eulogy is.

Who will give the eulogy? How many eulogies will you have? (Typically, one to three prepared eulogies can be given.)

_____

_____

_____

Will there be an opportunity for spontaneous remembrances from those gathered? If so, at which service may this occur and who will guide this part of the service?

_____

Are there parts of the service to which family members or friends can contribute? (For example, may a family member or friend read the readings or sing?)

_____

_____

_____

Personal Touches

Can visual mementos of the deceased be set up (pictures and/or personal belongings) for those attending to see? If so, where and when will they be set up?

_____

_____

Who will be responsible for seeing that the display is set up and taken down?

_____

_____

How long will the service be?

_____

Reception

Will there be a reception held after the service? Where will it be?

_____

_____

Who will prepare the refreshments/meal and set it up?

_____

_____

_____

Is there a fee for the reception? If so, how much will it cost?

_____

What restrictions, if any, does the place of worship have for a reception held after a funeral?

_____

_____

CHAPTER 6

It is important that we, who are left,
know that this life mattered to
ourselves and to others . . .

PERSONALIZING THE SERVICES

When a service is personalized, it is as if the very life breath of the individual is present. The service becomes an expression of our beliefs, hopes, sorrows, and comforts. The ritual does indeed fulfill its purpose to honor the deceased and provide comfort in our grief. Our rituals give us a safe harbor in which to give expression to the experience. It becomes important to most people that the service be a reflection of whom their loved one was. Personalizing the service allows for an opportunity to give expression to the joy of knowing the loved one as well as the sorrow of our loss.

There will be many decisions to make, and it takes time to sort out what you want to do and what you can do. During a time of loss, many people come forward to offer their help and assistance. Most of us welcome the support. Ask for help when you need it. The kindness of others will carry you through the difficult days. When preparing a service, we can be certain of only one thing: it will have the quality of the unexpected and probably will not be perfect. That's all right. It is not perfection we seek, but expression. Even under the best of circumstances, death sends our emotions on a rollercoaster ride. Feelings come and go, washing us in intensity one minute and numbing us the next.

The truth about grief is that during these initial days it stays with us and is present in every moment. A short impersonal service is not going to lessen the pain. A personalized service, long or short, traditional or not, gives us a place to acknowledge the sorrow in the presence of others. It also gives us the opportunity to see that the life of our loved one mattered. We are not alone in our loss. We honor the life of the one who has died and, in the telling of the story, in the readings and music we choose, we find comfort. The service helps us to be grounded in the present, to reflect on the past and to find solace so that we can move forward into the future.

The following thoughts, ideas, and examples are provided to give you a way to begin to think about how you want to personalize the services. You can add these personal touches to each of the services you have. You may use as much or as little of the information as you need.

Private Time

The private gathering for family and close friends can be held before the time set for the community to gather. This may be the first time some family members have seen their loved one since the death occurred. It is appropriate to touch the body of your loved one if you want. Family members may bring their children during this time, allowing them to touch the body and to ask questions about what has happened. If possible, have an adult available to answer the children's questions. Children generally accept the reality of death very quickly. Your openness with them helps them accept their loss. Children may draw pictures or say a few words. This private time is a unique setting for your expressions of grief.

You can place a special prayer book or memento in the casket if you wish. A simple prayer, poem, or reading, spoken or read at the end of your private time with the body, helps to signal an end to the family time. It will help prepare you to meet with the community. If you prefer more structure, you may use some prayers for gathering in the presence of the body. Be sure to talk with the leader of your religious tradition if you want help with this time. Ask to see some of the prayers and decide what your selections or choices might be.

Gathering with the Community

It is important to talk briefly about the period during which the community comes to pay their respects. Generally, the immediate family and significant others are the focus of this time. People come at this time to say their farewell to the deceased and to acknowledge their relationship to the family. Even though the body of the deceased may not be present, they are paying respect to the memory of their friend or family member. Often, people come to support a family member of the deceased even if they themselves were not close to the one who died.

In the case of a sudden or an unexpected death, this service can be overwhelming for the parents, spouse, or children of the deceased. It is helpful to have a good friend by your side to help take care of your needs at this time. A friend can get you a glass of water, help you find a chair to sit on, or stand with you in silence as you greet others. Friends do not shield us from grief but give support and comfort during a long and tiring time.

Even though the day is difficult emotionally, it is a day you will look back on and remember. It is a pivotal experience in your life. The outward expressions of the grief, such as tears of sadness, are a confirmation that death has come. The outpouring of love from your family and friends will comfort you, and give you strength in the long days ahead. Each individual has had their own relationship with the deceased and has their own process to go through to get to a place of acceptance. The more we allow ourselves the gift of that expression, the easier it is to let go of the deceased and to move on with our lives. The services allow us to integrate our feelings about the death as fully as we can.

Personal Contributions

You may ask family members or close friends to take a moment to share a memory, poem, or personal writing to be used before the conclusion of the visitation or vigil for the deceased. Ask people to contribute what they can or want. If you leave it open to them, they will respond.

At a grandfather's visitation, the grandchildren were offered an opportunity to share their memories of time with him. After some of them spoke, there was a spontaneous movement among his friends and associates who had come. One after another, they stood and told stories about fishing with him, camping, working, and living with him. Some of the stories were funny and added much laughter as they recalled moments in his life. Give people permission to express themselves and you will be surprised with what they do.

A woman's best friend was killed in a car accident. A friendship of thirty-some years changed in one day. As she boarded the plan to fly to her home town for the funeral, she thought about her friend, still in disbelief and shock about the accident and her death. She wanted to say something about her friend, so and she began writing her thoughts to give to the family. While all the family appreciated her gift, half wanted her to read it at the funeral and half felt it would be too emotional. They asked her to read her thoughts at the vigil the evening before the funeral.

Here are the thoughts she presented at the vigil:

> To you, Joce:
>
> My heart is filled with sadness today, for I must say farewell to my oldest and dearest friend. My sadness is not only for me, but for the loss to the world, for she is no longer with us.
>
> Oh Joce, how nice it would be to be with you today, even just for a while; to tell you that you have been a wonderful friend and to see your warm smile, the sparkle in your beautiful brown eyes, to hear you laugh. To update each other on what we have been doing, perhaps to reminisce a bit . . .
>
> It seems like only yesterday we met at the corner and walked to school together every day for twelve years. Remember all the hours we spent together, either in your room or in mine, talking about our loves, our heartaches, our families, our hopes, and our dreams.
>
> I can even recall getting into trouble together—like the time we got caught smoking in your playhouse and were grounded for a month. I still laugh when I think of you running down the alley in your nightgown with a mop when our basement was flooding. I can't remember any event of my childhood that you weren't a part of. You were dearly loved by all of my family. My mom used to speak not of her eight children, but of her nine children, because you were included.

A special memory is when you fell in love with Tyler, your first and only love. You were so happy. My heart overflowed with joy for you on your wedding day, as I watched you walk down the aisle with Tyler. It was always fun to share our experiences in raising children when we became moms.

Joce, there is so much I want to say to you today, but most of all I thank you for enriching my life with your friendship. As we both know, good friends, let alone best friends, are hard to find. We found each other and formed a best friendship that neither time nor distance could diminish.

During this difficult time, I realize how precious and far too rare are those people who cling to the best of values: loyalty, honesty, and love. You, my dear friend, truly lived by these values, and I will always respect and cherish you for that.

My heart is crying today, for I must go on without you, but the angels are smiling to have you with them. My best friend will be buried tomorrow, and the earth will weep. You were my friend, you are my friend, and you will always be my best friend . . .

Farewell. —Jane Miller

Provide some time and invite those gathered to speak their thoughts.

Meditations

You may choose a meditation to be used in the service. This can be a poem, a scripture reading, or other selection. It can be written by a friend or family member. Or it can be a time of silent prayer or reflection. Ask your religious leader or funeral director to find out when it is appropriate for you to have a meditation in the service. Most often, people use a meditation before the service begins. The following meditation was composed by a family member for their mother's funeral:

> God of all consolation, we come before you today,
> hearts full of sorrow. In your kindness look upon us as we say good-bye to our mother. In this lifetime we have shared many memories; create in us a place to remember all that is important. Help us to bring into your presence all that we hold dear, all that has been said and unsaid.
>
> We thank you for the gift of our mother, our friend,
> the gift of life freely given, the promise of life everlasting fulfilled. We ask for your compassion to sustain us, your light to illuminate our darkness, your peace to carry us gently in the days before us. Amen —J.M.

Eulogy

The eulogy is a time for personal reflection given by a member of the family or by a significant friend of the family. It can also be given by the leader of the service, if you prefer. When you or someone you ask will give the eulogy, it is important that you have enough time to prepare. Here is a eulogy given at the funeral service of a young man. His friends gathered the night before to share their thoughts and a few of them spoke at the service. The death was unexpected and this eulogy came from the heart, a spontaneous expression of their shock, grief, and love for the deceased.

> Dear Marty,
>
> There is a character in the book of Genesis who I'm beginning to associate with you as I sit and write. His name is Enoch, and he walked with God. Then God took him, and he wasn't.

The rabbis in the Talmud weren't satisfied with such a short narrative, so they built a mystical literature around him, saying that Enoch was transformed into an angel—in fact, the highest angel. When people sought their own experiential knowledge of God, they would encounter this Enoch, whose name became Metatron. God explained that of all of the angels in God's service, Enoch was the greatest, for he had been human—and could help other humans experience that which was beyond experience.

Marty, to me you were an angel on earth already. Your eyes always shone with the light of understanding, holding back fear, yet still vulnerable enough to feel. You listened to me and I listened to you. We communicated with an understanding and humor and love. And humor. Your ability to joke was by far your most angelic quality. You always seemed to be aware of how big life really was, how important and even how absurd, yet it did not prevent you from making others laugh and making yourself laugh.

In the last few years we got to know each other again as adults, more or less. We discussed relationships and Judaism and the law, and it seemed to me as though our new connection with each other was timed for just a short convergence. Short, but meaningful. I moved and you married. I anticipated many years of visits and recapitulations of what we'd been learning, who we're becoming, and when we'll connect again. And now you simply aren't. I had no idea how short our convergence would be. Though in the past I told you how much I appreciated you, I feel as though, were you able to read my words now, I could write volumes on the subject.

To Carolyn and Aimee, I know of no words which can comfort you at this time. There are none. I hope that Marty's love can envelop you as you feel what you will feel and that your community of friends and family can reflect his love, which we ourselves have experienced, back to you in support in these days and in the future.

Love, Barry

When you are writing your eulogy, it is helpful to prepare a few written remarks to help stay focused. You can refer to the suggested list of topics for a eulogy in this chapter. Here is another example of an expression said by a father at his son's funeral:

In reflecting upon Garrett's life as we say good-bye to his physical presence, I know that he would want me to say some special thank yous to those who flavored and touched his life:

All my aunts and uncles—
Thank you for spending the time you did with me and making such a fuss over my small accomplishments. I know when I was with you, I was the center of your attention. For that I have no regrets. In fact, I thoroughly enjoyed every minute of it. I have absorbed your love and will give back much more as you continue your journey to me.

Jack and Marg—
Thank you for caring for me through my illness. You eased my pain and made my discomfort as little as possible. You have a gift which brings love and strength to all my friends who are so sick. We are thankful you have chosen to share your special gift with us.

Great-grandpa and Great-grandma—
Thank you for allowing me to transcend the years, so that I may know your special love and beauty.

Grandpa Joe and Grandpa Doc—
Thank you for all you did to help Mommy and Daddy during the time of my illness. Continue to be a guide to them, even when they don't want it. Oh, one more thing. You'll be relieved to know that God is Irish.

I have a very special thank you to my Nana—
You were everything a grandson could wish for and much, much more. Thank you for all the time you gave me. Know that I am safe and well loved here. I will always be with you. Please talk with me often. I love you with all my soul.

Mommy—
You are the best mommy I could have desired. To be honest, Daddy and I weren't so sure how you would fare at this mommy business . . . (actually it was only Daddy). I knew how wonderful, loving and caring a mommy you would be. Although our time was short I never wanted for love and affection. You took such good care of me. Now I will help take care of you and Daddy.

Although there is much pain with Garrett's death, there is also much happiness. He gave us love and strength. He smiled through his suffering to ease ours. I am thankful for his time. He knew not rejection, despair, anger, or any of the pains that our world holds. He knew only of love, caring and affection. He is happy for this.

There is much to say of his time with us, but words have limitations that our sweet memories do not. And so I leave them untouched as Garrett made and nurtured them.

And now, from Mommy—
To a life filled with joy and laughter

mixed with suffering and sorrow
faced with courage and determination
and not a single moment wasted . . .
We love you, son. —T.S.M.

There is no set formula for the eulogy. A eulogy is an expression of your thoughts about the deceased. It can be brief or detailed. The content of the eulogy depends on the person giving this gift of remembrance. You may also include thoughts or remarks from the deceased. If you are planning the service before the death occurs, the person who is terminally ill may have some remarks they would like to share. Conversations with the dying person reveal what readings are important to them or what songs they would like to have played. They may have even written a piece that reflects their thoughts about their life that they wish to be included in the service. These conversations can be incorporated into the service.

Blessings

You may want to include a blessing that comes from your cultural heritage. Ask the leader of your religious tradition or funeral director if this is allowed and where it is appropriate to use it in the service. This blessing can be read by a family member or friend just before the closing of the service. Remember that the final blessing is provided by the religious tradition, coming from the ritual itself.

You may write your own or others in your circle of family and friends may want to write a blessing that would be used before the final blessing provided by the church. Ask for help. There are no rules for prayers, most simply come from the heart out of our experiences. Trust in your abilities or those of others.

Here is an example of an Irish blessing:

> May the blessings of light be upon you, light without and light within.
> May the blessed sunlight shine on you and warm your heart till it glows
> like a great peat fire, so that the stranger may come and warm himself by
> it, and also a friend. And may the light shine out of the two eyes of you
> like a candle set in two windows of a house, bidding the wanderer to
> come in out of the storm.
>
> And may the blessings of the rain be upon you—the soft sweet rain. May
> it fall upon your spirit so that all the little flowers may spring up and shed
> their sweetness on the air. And may the blessings of the great rains be on
> you: may they beat upon your spirit and wash it fair and clean, and leave
> there many a shining pool where the blue of heaven shines reflected, and
> sometimes a star.
>
> And may the blessings of the earth be upon you—the great and round
> earth. May you ever have a kindly greeting for them you pass as you're
> going along the roads. May the earth be soft under you when you lie upon
> it, tired at the end of the day. And may it rest easy over you when at last
> you lie out under it. May it rest so lightly over you that your soul may be
> quickly through it, and on its way to God.

Personal Touches

There will be time for the community to gather at the service. Take a moment now
to think about which mementos you want displayed and how they will be displayed. At a memorial service for a young woman, for example, an enlarged picture
was placed at the front of the church. Flowers were set all around it. At another
service the sail from the man's favorite boat hung on the back wall like a banner.

For one young family whose child died during birth, the tiny coffin used for the child was made by a friend who was a woodworker. Even though the time is short, people can and do respond to these special requests. Most people feel it is an honor to help contribute and are more than happy to help.

Ask the funeral director or place of worship if you may use mementos in the church or at the funeral home during the service. Some religious traditions may not allow personal effects to be used during the funeral service but do allow them to be used at the wake, vigil or visitation, and reception. You should speak with the worship leader to determine when this is appropriate.

You can set out photographs of your loved one in a display that shows the history of the person. Baby pictures, family albums, graduation photos, casual pictures, and mementos of accomplishments can be set out. They can be arranged on one or more tables. Walking sticks, pipes, hats, uniforms, posters, books, things made by your loved one, certificates of accomplishments or other important memorabilia are all appropriate for the display. In the case of a child, you may include a favorite toy, sporting equipment, art projects they made, or other objects of affection in the display.

The family can compile the photos and objects before the service. Each picture or object will evoke a story or memory that we will carry with us for the rest of our lives. They are outward expressions of what was important to the person who has just died and tell some of the story of his or her life. Photos placed on a bulletin board or tables serve as a visible reminder, and give focus to the story we are telling. Some funeral homes will create a videotape for you made from family photographs you give them. Or you can play music on a tape or CD player in the background of your photo display. You may want to check with the funeral home or church to see if they will provide music for the background. If they do not, ask if you can bring your own music system to use at this time.

Flowers

Flowers are often sent by family and friends in acknowledgment of the death. These flowers can be arranged around the casket or near the entryway of the church or the funeral home. Generally, the funeral director will arrange the flowers. You may request a specific type of flower arrangement. You can order the flowers yourself from a florist or request that the funeral home purchase them for you. The cost of the flowers you request is your responsibility.

In many cases an estate is paying for the funeral cost, but some estates will not cover the expense of flowers. This is defined as a gift or expression from the family. Probate may tend to see the cost of the flowers as a family expense.

Memorial Cards

If you want to design your memorial card, but need help with the printing, let the funeral director know that. He or she can help you get the cards printed. Designing the memorial card provides a way to add a personal touch to the public record of death. Very often someone from the place of worship is available to help you create a personalized program in much the same way that programs are printed for weddings.

There are many different ways to add a personal touch to the memorial card. One family had a photo of the family farm on the back of the memorial card for their mother. Another family had the memorial card folded with a photo of their daughter on one side with a favorite poem included. A favorite quote or thought that represents the deceased can be printed on the front of the card. One father wrote a five-line tribute to his daughter and included it on the inside of her memorial card.

It is simple to design your card. There are many printing centers and copy stores available. You can easily produce them in time for the service. The possibilities are endless and come out of your own experience. The front of the card can have a photograph or drawing or simple quotation or symbol. The back of the card includes the name, date of birth and death, date and place of service, and burial site. Some include a verse from scripture or a note of farewell. Some people choose to create a small card with a symbol on the front, with information in the middle and a photo on the back.

Printed Programs

You may choose to have a program printed. This is fairly easy once you have chosen the content of the service. You can use the same design from the memorial card, if you want, or you can choose something different. Once you have selected the cover for the program, you can create the content of the program based on the selections of music and readings you have made and have copies made before the funeral service.

The program can list by name the survivors, readers, musicians, and pallbearers. It can include the eulogy or a written message from the deceased. It can be copied quickly at a print shop. Ask those around you to help. One young woman did the artwork for the cover of the program for her husband's funeral. The death was unexpected, but she wanted to take her love of art and drawing to make a final tribute to her husband.

These personal touches have great meaning for all involved and give family and friends something concrete to do. Look to yourselves and your circle of friends for these experiences. Ask, ask, ask. People want to help. There are many who can.

Music and Readings

When you talk with the place of worship about the services, ask if the church has musicians available to participate in the service. Most do. If not, you may choose to hire musicians to play and/or sing at the service(s). Whoever you choose can assist you in the selection of music. You may also request a copy of the church hymnal to help you find those songs that have meaning for you.

During your meeting with the place of worship or with the funeral director you will have been given information about the selection of readings. Once you have chosen the readings and selected or written the intercessory prayers or meditation, you can go over this material with the musicians. They will be able to guide you to musical selections that will complement the material you have chosen. By allowing others to help you plan the service, you will find that their ideas will give an added dimension to the service.

The music can be played before, during, or after the service as people are leaving. You may select music that your loved one enjoyed during life or music that your family enjoys. Music is soothing. It touches our hearts and gives solace as it eases our tension and speaks to our tired bodies and hearts at this time.

Pallbearers

Will you have pallbearers? As a practical consideration, most caskets are heavy. Sometimes the selection of the pallbearers has to do with the ability to lift and carry the heavy weight of the casket. Physical strength and possibly a strong back may be necessary for this task. Pallbearers act as an honor guard for the casket. Usually these are the children, grandchildren, friends, or associates of the deceased. They help carry the casket in and escort the casket out of the service. Honorary pallbearers are not required to actually lift and carry the casket. Usually there is a minimum of four to six pallbearers.

Burial Services

The body, present in either the casket or in the cremation urn, is set in place for the burial. Some people choose to add a reading of poetry or section from an author that had special meaning to the deceased or to the family. These selections can be read by a family member or close friend. You may choose to read a short blessing or note of farewell that you have written. These can be included in addition to the prayers and readings provided by the church. One person wrote this short farewell that was read at the burial service:

> Lay to rest the physical remains of my beloved:
> No longer beside me, forever within me, I let you go. Released from the
> world into that which I cannot see, close to my heart. —J.M.

The place or worship may provide musicians for the graveside service or you may choose to hire musicians. One family had bagpipes play at the service. Another chose a simple piece of flute music. You may use an instrumental piece of music in addition to a song. Some people decide to release balloons as a symbol of releasing the spirit of the loved one. These choices are personal and many find a sense of completion in these final actions.

Family members and significant others may put the first shovel of dirt on the casket or urn after it is lowered into the ground. You may also invite others present to participate. It is up to your wishes and desires in this matter. Some families choose to leave the cemetery after the service but before the casket or urn is lowered into the ground. Some choose to stay and help with the actual burial of the body. Choose whatever is appropriate and helpful for you.

Once these details are addressed and taken care of you can breathe a little easier. Your work is complete. By this time your body is tired. Allow the service and ceremony to help you. Let it speak to you and ease the sorrow a bit.

Questions to Consider

When planning the service it is important to keep in mind that there may be differences in peoples thoughts and feelings about what type of service to have or what should be included. Be respectful of one another's differences.

Will the casket be open or closed during the vigil?

_____

Do you want a private time for the family and close friends to spend with the body? If so, how much private time do you want? (One half-hour or more?)

_____

_____

Personalizing the Wake, Visitation, or Vigil for the Deceased

What mementos do you want to place in the casket?

_____

_____

_____

Do you have a poem, psalm, reading, prayer, meditation, or song you would like read or sung? List them here.

_____

_____

_____

Will you have time for personal contributions from friends or family? Invite those gathered to speak their thoughts. Who will speak at this time?

_____

_____

_____

How long will the community portion of the wake/visitation/vigil last?

_____

Do you want to create a photo display? If so, who will bring it to the service?

_____

93

Do you want to display mementos of the deceased? If so, what are they and who will help assemble them and set up the display?

_____

_____

_____

How much space will you need for the display(s) and where will they be set up?

_____

_____

Memorial Cards

What do you want on the front of the card? Perhaps a picture of the deceased or a favorite quotation or scripture verse? A quotation, saying, or symbol is also appropriate.

_____

_____

What are your thoughts for the back of the memorial card here. Do you want to include a photo, a note of farewell, artwork?

_____

_____

Who will print it or take it to be copied and how many copies do you want?

_____

_____

The memorial cards are generally set out by the guest book for people to take a copy. Many people save these as a memento of the deceased. The front of the memorial card may also be used as the cover of the funeral program.

Funeral Programs

Do you want a funeral program? If so, what will it include?

_____

_____

_____

Do you want the program to include the entire service? The text of the readings, and songs—as well as listing the readers, musicians, or pallbearers—can be included.

_____

_____

Printing deadline for the program:

_____

Flowers

Flowers that you order can be used at both the visitation or vigil for the deceased and the funeral service.

Do you want any specific flowers?

_____

Who will order them?

_____

Personalizing the Funeral or Memorial Service

Who will help to place the pall(cloth) on the casket?

_____

Will you use a meditation before the service begins? Will it be written or selected from an existing source?

_____

Have you selected the readings to used in the service?

_____

Do you want to write the prayers to be used in the service? Who will help you?

_____

Music for the Service(s)

You will possibly be selecting music for two services if you have both a vigil and a funeral. You may use music to signal the beginning and/or the end of the service for the vigil for the deceased. In some circumstances you may not be using musicians at the vigil but instead may select to use recorded music.

Is a sound system provided by the funeral home or church? If not, do you want to bring your tape or CD player?

_____

What recorded music have you selected?

_____

_____

Who is in charge of choosing and playing the selections?

_____

Have you selected music that was special to your loved one?

_____

Does the church have musicians available for the service? Are you asking a friend to sing or play an instrument or are you hiring musicians for any of this?

For which service(s)?

_____

_____

Whom have you selected? List their name(s) and phone number(s):

_____

_____

What music have you selected for the services?

_____

_____

_____

Be sure to tell the musicians you hire the time, date, and location of the service.

At what times will they play for the visitation/wake?

_____

_____

At what times will they play for the funeral/memorial service?

_____

_____

Will musicians play at the graveside services? At what times?

_____

_____

What music have you selected?

_____

_____

_____

Eulogy and Personal Contribution

When you are writing your eulogy, it is helpful to prepare a few written remarks to help start. You may also include thoughts or remarks from the deceased.

Following is a list of thoughts you may consider including in the eulogy:

- historical remarks such as: date and place of birth, place in the family (oldest, youngest, etc.)
- name of parents
- education/training
- accomplishments
- personal essence
- memories of time spent together
- significant relationships
- passions and activities involved in, such as sports, theater, causes, etc.

Meditations, Prayers, and Blessings

Do you have a meditation, blessing and/or prayer you would like to use?

_____

_____

_____

Who will read each of these: religious leader, family member, significant friend?

_____

_____

_____

What service(s) will these be used in?

_____

_____

_____

Graveside Services

Who will be the pallbearers?

_____

_____

_____

_____

Will the graveside services be a private time for the family and invited guests only?

_____

Is there a favorite poem or verse that you would like read at the graveside service?

_____

_____

Do you have a blessing that you would like to use or write to be given before the final committal blessing of the church?

_____

_____

Do you want the family to stay (if you are preplanning) or will you stay for the lowering of the casket or urn into the ground? Will you or others shovel the dirt? Will you stay until the burial is complete?

_____

_____

CHAPTER 7

When we plan the details of the service,
we can fully embrace and experience the
funeral as an expression of our grief,
hope, and joy of having lived
with our beloved . . .

Nontraditional Services

Funerals and memorials are a family affair. We come together, in the end, to give a final farewell to the presence of our beloved. Each of us, in our own way, comes to terms with the meaning of our relationships and the path our grief takes. It is important to remember that the purpose of the service is not only to honor the life of the one who has died, but to provide comfort for those of us left behind. Whether you practice a certain religious belief or not, the funeral ceremonies are really a reflection of spiritual beliefs. The rituals we use provide the structure for us as we find ways to give expression to the meaning of our lives with our beloved and give voice to the beliefs we hold for ourselves.

Decisions about the Type and Location of Services

Because you have decided that you will not use a structure provided by a faith tradition, you must decide what services you will have and who will lead them. Basically you can have a visitation, funeral or memorial service, and burial service or disposition of the cremated remains. You must decide if you will have the services at the funeral home, cremation society, home or other location. You will need to designate a leader for the services, someone who will make sure the service has a focus for the beginning, middle, and end of the service. Many people ask the funeral director to help with this task. Some select a family member or close friend to work with the funeral director in leading the service. This chapter will help you plan the services you will use if you are not using a religious framework.

Designing the Visitation or Wake

Designing the structure for vigil or visitation service yourself is not a complicated task. This service can be lead by the funeral director, family member, or friend of the deceased. Designing the service will require some organization about the content of what you want to include. Remember that this service is not the funeral service. The service is a simple one. Use that as your guiding principle as you think about what you want to do. An outline of a simple service is provided here as an example of what you can include in a service.

- invitation to gather
- song or Instrumental music
- reading (can be religious or nonreligious)
- sharing stories or memories
- blessing or prayers said for the deceased
- closing thoughts/music

Designing the Funeral

If you are designing the service yourself, you may be asked to think of prayers you want used or you may ask to include them yourself. You may write your own, or others in your circle of family and friends may want to compose them. You may select prayers from prayer books or other sources that have meaning for you. Ask for help. There are no rules for prayers. Most prayers simply come from the heart, out of your experience. Trust in your abilities or those of others. The words will come, simply and beautifully. Remember this is a time for you. Each one of us communicates in a unique and individual way. Give voice to what is in your heart. Do as much as you can to put meaning into the service. Make the most of this opportunity. It comes only once. Because you are not using a traditional religious framework it is helpful to prepare an outline for the funeral service. An outline for the service is provided at the end of this chapter.

Planning the Service

The following pages contain information which will help you with decisions regarding the content of the services.

Invocation

An invocation is the act of calling people together to begin the service. It can be written by you or another. Here is an example of an invocation:

> We gather today as a community of family and friends to honor the life
> and memory of [insert the name of the deceased]. In the sadness of our
> grief, we come to share the stories we hold dear to our hearts. We
> remember and honor the gifts that were shared, the times we had togeth-
> er and the beliefs we hold. In this time of sorrow, we look to one another

to affirm the place [he/she] has made in our lives and the memories we carry into the future without them. We have selected readings and music to help give form to our thoughts and invite you to share your thoughts as well. Let us take a moment of silence to prepare.

Music

You will need to determine how many songs you want to include and if any of the selections will be instrumental. If you have music that was especially enjoyed by your loved one you can select that. You may use music to signal the beginning and end of the service. Music speaks to us on many levels. Often, the melodies ease our hearts and minds when we have been in difficult circumstances. The music you select, those songs, hymns, or verses that are dear to you, should also help to uplift and sustain you during the service. Music helps us give voice to what is in our hearts that mere words can not convey. Allow the selections to provide a soothing balm for your grief. For specific information about selection of music you may refer to chapter 6.

Readings or Meditations

When you are selecting the readings, you should decide how many will be used. You may use poetry or readings from a favorite book or author. Some people use a selection from the Bible, *The Book of Common Prayer*, the Koran, or some other inspirational book. You may want to include a short meditation that is read before the leader begins the service. Ask if it is appropriate for you to have a meditation in the service. The meditation can be read by a family member or friend. A meditation can be a psalm, a quote, or a writing composed by a family or a friend. It is a time in the service to focus our thoughts on what our loved one has meant to us. The following example of a meditation, written by a young man after his wife died suddenly, reflects his beliefs about his wife's life and the meaning he struggled to understand from her passing:

> With a loss like this so deep and telling, we are isolated in our sadness, transfixed in our grief.
>
> We seek help, strength, support. We seek reasons for why this happened and there are none at hand.
>
> It is then that we must reach within ourselves, individually and collectively, and we must remember:
>
> We must remember Jocelyn: vibrant, alive, filled with energy. And something else: a commitment to her family, to her friends, to her community.
>
> There was a driving force in her life of commitment. It was her Christian faith, her belief that God would watch over her and over us.
>
> Jocelyn's credo was based in the fact that a love of God would reflect itself in a love and understanding of our own human condition. It was founded in her knowledge that her good example could reflect a positive response in those who were so much a part of her life.
>
> This philosophy, this objective of Jocelyn's, was accomplished with a simplicity of purpose etched in true dedication.
>
> Really, it is what each of us are taught. And what she was taught she put into practice in her life.
>
> That is so meaningful to each of us now. It gives us that sense of comfort we search for, because we, above all, know that God takes care of his children on earth when their time comes to be with Him.

We are confident that Jocelyn, through her corporal works on earth, now is with the God she loved, watching over us, helping to guide us, and at the same time, beginning a life of true happiness and fulfillment with her Savior in his Kingdom of happiness.

This is what she strived for in her years with us. This is what we believe.
—T.F.

Eulogy

The eulogy is given by a family member or friend. You will need to ask the individual(s) you have chosen to prepare some written remarks to be read at the service. For specific information about and examples of eulogies you may refer to chapter 6.

Remembrances

This is a time to invite those present to share a story or thoughts about the deceased. It differs from the eulogy because you have not specifically requested an individual to speak. This is a place for spontaneous sharing from those gathered. For examples of personal contributions you may refer to chapter 6.

Blessings

The blessing is used as a way to formally end the service. It is the final farewell to the deceased and helps to put closure to the funeral service. A blessing is an expression of hope, love, and faith that we give to the one who has died. We remember them as they were and use our words to help release them from this time and place. They take a journey on which we cannot go. We need to release our hold on them, both for ourselves and them. A blessing is just a heartfelt Godspeed, good luck that we give in ordinary days, but in the days of sorrow it takes on a special meaning as it is the final farewell.

The blessing may be written by a family member or friend and read by the individual who is leading the service. For example:

> We bless the body of (name of deceased) with full hearts and open hands. We are grateful for our time spent together. Memories held and experiences shared, we stand in the presence of those who have gathered to say farewell. We wish you dear [name], peace on your journey. Released from this life, our love and care go with you. Godspeed.

Another example of a blessing can be found in chapter 6.

Graveside Services or Ceremony to Scatter the Ashes

The graveside service consecrates or blesses the ground before burial. The service is brief and can include a reading of scripture or poetry. The family may stay while the burial is complete and help with the burial if desired. Some may decide to leave before the actual burial is completed. Ideas for personalizing this service are found in chapter 6. If you will be scattering the ashes you will have decided where this will take place. It is important to remember that this final act of releasing our loved one is a sacred time and care should be taken to make this service meaningful for the survivors.

Outline for Designing a Funeral or Memorial Service

Invocation
Music to call people together
Reading or meditation (from a favorite poet, scripture, or passage from a book)
Eulogy (given by a family member or close friend)
Remembrances
Readings or prayers
Blessings or final commendation (farewell to the deceased)
Music or meditation to complete the service

Questions to Consider

These are to be used only if you are not using a specific faith tradition's framework for the service. You can use these questions to help think about some of the content of the service. Other ideas for personal touches can be found in chapter 6.

What type(s) of service(s) will be held?

_____

Who will lead the service(s)?

_____

Where will the service(s) be held?

_____

What type of burial will be used?

_____

Will a graveside ceremony be used or a ceremony to scatter the ashes? Where?

_____

_____

Do you wish to use a meditation or reading to begin the service? If so, what will it be? If composing an original, who will write it?

_____

Will you have an invocation? Who will write it? Who will read it?

_____

How many readings will you need? List them here:

_____

_____

How many places for music will there be within the service? Do you need an entrance song, or songs in between, a closing song? List the songs here:

_____

_____

Will you hire musicians to sing or to play an instrument? List musicians here:

_____

_____

Be sure to tell them the time, date, and location of the service.

CHAPTER 8

Gently the music fades, and the soothing
arms of a friend or loved one embraces us.
Sharing food and conversations,
we move forward in the company
of friends and family.

AFTER THE SERVICES

After the service at the burial place is completed, family, friends, and community members may gather for a reception or for the memorial service, in which case the reception follows. It is like a sigh of relief. The reception is an unstructured event that family and friends can use as an opportunity to unwind in the presence of people who care about them. It is an opportunity to eat together, to converse with one another, and to give one another comfort and encouragement. For some places of worship this is the appropriate time and place for displaying the mementos and personal touches you wanted to include.

Reception

The reception is a time for sharing a meal. It is a more relaxed time for all of us. Preparing for the funeral and the burial takes so much emotional energy and effort. We are often left with little or no time to sit and let down a bit in the days following the death. The reception is a time to be with one another. It gives us time to acknowledge that life continues even in the midst of death.

The reception is generally hosted by members of the church or by close family friends. However, for some communities the cost of food has become so expensive that congregation members are able to donate their time to help organize the reception and serve the food. They ask the family to cover the actual costs. Those who help organize the reception serve the food, host the reception, and clean up afterward. This is a valuable service to the family. It is truly a gift to the family.

If you are not using a place of worship or funeral home for the reception, it can be held at the home of a family member or friend, or at a banquet hall. The event can be catered if you want. The family usually pays for the costs of the event. You can ask someone to help you by hosting the reception. Again, most people are honored to help. Leave the details of the reception for them to handle or, if you want to, you can coordinate the details with them.

Thank-You Notes

Often during the funeral we are unaware of the many actions and activities of others because all our energy is spent trying to get through the service. The writing of thank-you notes gives us a chance to go back and see what we were unable to see at the time.

The thank-you notes serve two purposes. First, they acknowledge the flowers, gifts, memorials, or other help given during the preparations for the funeral. Second, they give us another opportunity to again reconnect with others. There is not a prescribed period for the sending of thank-you notes. However, they should generally be sent a short time after the services are completed. The funeral home may have a selection of thank-you notes to chose from. You can also buy thank-you notes or have some printed for you. You may choose to use the cover of the memorial card or program for the cover of the thank-you notes, leaving it blank inside for your message. You may choose to create your own thank-you card with a reading, poem, or note, or select one that is ready made.

Some choose to send thank-you notes, some do not. Certainly, most people would say they do not expect them, let alone view them as a requirement. The acts of kindness extended to us during a time of sorrow are spontaneous and greatly appreciated. Sending a note of thanks, although not required, is a simple way of acknowledging the many gifts received during a difficult time.

Questions to Consider

Where will the reception be held?

_____

_____

How long will the reception last?

_____

Who is responsible for making the arrangements?

_____

_____

Do you want the photo display or mementos used at the reception? If so, who is responsible setting these up and taking them down?

_____

_____

What is the fee, if any, for the reception?

_____

Do you want to send thank-you notes? Will you design your own thank-you notes?

_____

_____

Out of unrest to rest.
Out of disorder to order.
Grief cuts a new path,
moving us through the chaos
toward healing.

EPILOGUE

What funeral rituals offer us is the opportunity to begin to put closure on the relationship that has ended and to incorporate the loss into existing relationships. The intense emotional reactions of sorrow, fear, and disorientation come unbidden, swiftly taking over, filling us with the memories of a life together. It becomes difficult to sort out how to address the details of a funeral when our heart and mind are filled with the sights and sounds of days gone by, intruded upon by the demands of the present.

The days after the death occurs are filled with moving back and forth between what was and is no more and the reality of the present. At times the process is overwhelming and grief seems to wash over us, drenching us with its intensity. The vacant stares of the bereaved, the forgetfulness, and the tears and the anger all give expression to the deep sorrow that fills the heart. At times the grief recedes, and we regain some sense of balance and calm. The ebb and flow of this immediate grief reaction varies for each of us. For the deceased, death is a release from this life. For the living, death is a dramatic shift in our reality, forcing a reorganization because we have no choice but to move forward.

There is a tendency in modern life to move quickly through our experiences. The demands of living push at us, and we push ourselves and others to move through our grief, put it behind us, and move on. The difficulty with death is that its intensity stops us in our tracks, shaking the very foundation we have built our lives upon.

The loss of a parent signals a change in generations. The one we have known all our lives is with us no more. We become the oldest living survivors, the front line for the generations that follow. The loss of a sibling signals a time when our peers are leaving us, moving us closer toward our own death. The loss of a spouse or a companion breaks a bond that has provided stability and security. The death of a child causes chaos and disruption, as it is out of the natural order of things, shattering our hopes and dreams for the future.

Death touches us all in many ways and in many forms. Each death of a loved one or someone close to us causes us to examine the purpose and meaning of life. The period of adjustment begins immediately after the death and continues well into the year or two following the death. The first two years after the death encompass the task of regaining some balance. A natural decrease in the intensity of the loss occurs over time. Each day, month, or year brings more release from our pain and trauma. The loss becomes more bearable.

The time following a death can be a stressful period. It is more stressful for some than for others. It is wise to extend gentleness and kindness to yourself, as well as to those around you during these days of sorrow. Few of us express our grief or sorrow in exactly the same way. Make an effort to be compassionate with yourself and with those around you during this time. The stress and strain experienced by those grieving the loss of a loved one will be eased if everyone involved makes a conscious effort to allow each person to grieve in their own way. There are no easy answers. Sometimes there are only difficult questions. All that is required is that we attempt to face our loss and to gently give it a voice.

Life, death, and resurrection.
In the presence of this
mystery, hope takes us
toward faith and moves
us forward.

ROMAN CATHOLIC RITUALS

The Catholic Church has allowed the use of cremation since 1963. The Church requires that the cremated remains be buried with the full graveside service rituals used at the time of burial. Scattering the ashes or keeping the ashes in an urn without burial is not approved by the Church. The funeral rites used by the Catholic Church are: the Vigil for the Deceased, the Funeral Liturgy, and the Rite of Committal (the burial service). Scripture selections used in the funeral rites of the Catholic Church are selected from the New American Bible with Revised New Testament. Your parish or pastoral minister will assist you is finding the correct text to be used.

The Vigil for the Deceased is a gathering time for family and friends of the deceased. The body of the deceased may be present or not and this time for informal gathering and remembering can be held the day before the funeral service or a few hours before the funeral service. This gathering is usually brought to a close with a selected reading from scripture, a time of personal reflections given by family members and friends, and a prayer or hymn to end the service.

The Funeral Service can be a Funeral Mass, a celebration of the Mass that includes the presence of the body; or a Memorial Mass, a celebration of the Mass that does not include the presence of the body. Often the burial of the body is concluded before a Memorial Mass. You may also have a funeral service that does not include the celebration of the Mass.

The following is an outline for the structure of the Mass. A * indicates the parts of the Liturgy that you can make the selections that will be used or indicates the option to have a family member participate.

A member of the Pastoral Ministry Team will guide you through the task of planning the Mass. You will be asked to select the music, readers for the scripture selections you have chosen, and the Intercessary prayers. The Sacred Scripture Texts found are those generally used in funeral services provided by the Catholic Church.

The Funeral Mass

- Prelude Music* — Placement of the Pall* (covers the casket)
- Gathering Song*
- 1st Reading* (selected from the Old Testament)
- Responsorial Psalm* (can be recited or sung)
- 2nd Reading* (selected from the Old or New Testament)
- Gospel acclamation
- Gospel Reading* (selected from Matthew, Mark, Luke, or John)
- Homily (Notes on the deceased's life are helpful to the person who is giving the homily.)
- Intercessions* (These prayers can be written and read by the family or close friends of the deceased. These are simple requests or prayers of thanksgiving and

are followed by the response, "Lord, hear our prayer." Usually three or four prayers are said.)

- Preparation of the Gifts* — Music for the Preparation* (Family members or friends may bring the gifts to the altar.)
- Holy Holy/Memorial Acclamation/Great Amen/Lamb of God (You may select Eucharist Ministers to assist with Communion)
- Communion Song*
- Meditation (optional, can be music or reading)*
- Final Commendation: In Paradisum (sung or recited)
- Closing Song*

If a Eulogy is to be given it is appropriate to wait until the conclusion of the Mass. The Eulogy may be given by family members or close friend. It is important to discuss the Eulogy with the priest or pastoral minister who is helping to coordinate the service.

The Rite of Committal (Burial Service)

Invitation
- Scripture Verse*
- Prayer over the Place of Committal
- Intercessions*
- The Lord's Prayer
- Concluding Prayer
- Prayer over the People
- Song to Conclude the Rite (optional)*

Ideas for personalizing these services appear in chapter 6.

Sacred Scriptures

The following scriptures are often used in Catholic services for the dead. (This material originally appeared in the *New American Bible with Revised New Testament*.)

Funerals for Adults

Old Testament Readings
1. Job 19:1,23–27
2. Isaiah 25:6,7–9
3. Lamentations 3:17–26
4. Daniel 12:1–3
5. 2 Maccabees 12:43–46

New Testament Readings
1. Acts 10:34–43 or 10:34–36, 42–43
2. Romans 5:5–11
3. Romans 5:17–21
4. Romans 6:3–9 or 6:3–4, 8–9
5. Romans 8:14–23
6. Romans 8:31–35, 37–39
7. Romans 14:7–9, 10–12
8. 1 Corinthians 15:20–24, 25–28
9. 1 Corinthians 15:51–57
10. 2 Corinthians 5:1, 6–10
11. Phillippians 3:20–21
12. 1 Thessalonians 4:13–18
13. 2 Timothy 2:8–13
14. 1 John 3:1–2
15. 1 John 3:14–16
16. Revelation 14:13
17. Revelation 20:11–21:1
18. Revelation 21:1–5, 6–7

Gospel Readings
1. Matthew 5:1–12
2. Matthew 11:25–30
3. Matthew 25:1–13
4. Matthew 25:31–46
5. Mark 15:33–39; 16:1–6
6. Luke 7:11–17
7. Luke 12:35–40
8. Luke 23:33, 39–43
9. Luke 23:44–49, 24: 1–6
10. Luke 24:13–35 or 24:13–16, 28–35
11. John 6:37–40
12. John 6:51–58
13. John 11:17–27 or 11:21–27
14. John 11:32–45
15. John 12:23–28 or 12:23–26
16. John 14:1–6
17. John 17:24–26

Funerals for Baptized Children

Old Testament Readings
1. Isaiah 25, 6, 7–9
2. Lamentations 3, 17–26

New Testament Readings
1. Romans 6:3–4, 8–9
2. Romans 14:7–9
3. 1 Corinthians 15:20–23
4. Ephesians 1:3–5
5. 1 Thessalonians 4:13–14,18
6. Revelation 7:9–10, 15–17
7. Revelation 21:1, 3–5

Gospel Readings
1. Matthew 11:25–30
2. John 6:37–40
3. John 6:51–58
4. John 11:32–38, 40

We are not alone. Tradition teaches this.
We come together to sit with one another, to
honor our loved one and to provide comfort
to those who mourn. "May God comfort
you among the other mourners
of Zion and Jerusalem."

JEWISH TRADITIONS

Burial usually occurs within twenty-four hours after the death occurs. The Jewish burial rituals begin with the preparation of the body and the funeral. This signals the start of many rituals that last a full eleven months following the death. The custom of *keri'ah* (a tear made in the mourner's outer garment made at the moment of death or at the funeral) symbolizes the extreme disruption that death has brought to the mourner's relationship with the deceased loved one. This will be worn throughout the week of Shiva, which begins when the mourner returns home from the burial. The funeral service can be brief or long. The focus is on honoring the life of the deceased.

Funeral Service

The following is a general outline of funeral services, recognizing that the specific components provided by the three major Jewish traditions may vary.

The service begins with the cutting of the ribbon *(keri'ah)* and can be done privately with the family before the service begins or publicly with the family in the presence of the congregation. Music may be used before the start of the service.

- Introductory Reading/Psalms (can be read in Hebrew and/or English)
- The most commonly used Psalms are Psalms 23 or 90. The thirty-first chapter of the book of Proverbs can be used in the funeral for a woman.
- Eulogy (notes about the deceased's life are helpful, family and/friends can speak in addition to the rabbi)

Memorial Prayer—El Molei Rachamim (meaning "God Full of Mercy")
- If the service in the synagogue the congregation accompanies the coffin to the graveside service.

Graveside Service
- Readings (there can be several readings)—Psalm 91 is frequently used
- Lowering and covering of the coffin
- Recitation of Mourners Kaddish

Shiva is the formal mourning ritual of the Jewish religion. Comforting the family begins with Shiva, a period of mourning lasting up to seven days. During this time, the family suspends all routine activity and the week is spent in prayer and mourning. Members of the community gather in the family's home to recite the Mourners *Kaddish* —a prayer proclaiming God's presence in our lives. After the ritual is concluded, food is provided for the family by the community of friends that have come to comfort the mourners and to mourn with them. The mourner lights a memorial *(Yahrzeit)* candle that will burn throughout the Shiva period. A *minyan*, a religious quorum of ten, is gathered to recite the Kaddish.

The rituals of mourning do not end with the completion of Shiva. On the one-year anniversary of the death, a marker is set at the grave site with a prayer service that marks the end of the year of mourning. Every year thereafter, on the anniversary known as *Yahrzeit*, the family lights a twenty-four-hour candle in honor of the deceased. At synagogue, the Kaddish is recited.

Personal Thoughts about Jewish Services

The following is a means for gathering the basic information for the services and burial arrangements that will be made.

Name:

_____

Hebrew Name:

_____

ben/bat (son/daughter of):

_____

Residence:

_____

_____

List immediate living relatives:

_____

_____

_____

_____

Funeral Arrangements (check if selected) *indicates in accordance with Jewish law

_____ Please bury me in a modest wooden casket.*

_____ I do not want to be embalmed unless necessary.*

_____ I would like my privacy respected by not being viewed by any relative or guest at my funeral.*

_____ I do not want to be made up by a cosmetologist*

_____ I want to be dressed in shroud/clothing.

If clothing, please specify: _____

_____ I want the family to try to remain until the conclusion of the internment (lowering) service.*

_____ I do not want to be cremated.*

_____ I would like the following rabbi(s) and cantor(s) to officiate if available:

_____

If possible I would like the following to serve as casket bearers:

_____

_____

Please mention the following about me:
I have been a member of the following clubs and organizations:

_____

_____

I have the following hobbies and interests:

_____

_____

These aspects of my personality I would like mentioned:

_____

_____

APPENDIX 3

The expression of our faith is found in the
traditions we use. We embrace what is
familiar, finding comfort in the rituals
provided by our beliefs. These rituals help
us to lift our hearts to the Creator,
the One from whom all life flows.

SUGGESTED BIBLE READINGS

JOB 19:23-27

I know that my Redeemer lives

PSALM 16:5-11

The Lord has assigned me my portion

PSALM 23

The Lord is my shepherd

PSALM 27:1,4-9,13,14,

The Lord is my light and my salvation

PSALM 31:1-3,9,10,14-17A, 24

My times are in your hands

PSALM 32:1-7

Transgressions are forgiven

PSALM 34:1-9,17-19,22

A righteous man may have many troubles

PSALM 36:7-10

The fountain of life

PSALM 42:1-6A,9-11

Put your hope in God

PSALM 46:1-5,10,11

God is our refuge and strength

PSALM 50:15

Call on me in the day of trouble

PSALM 71:1-3,17-21

You will restore my life

PSALM 90:1–12

Teach us to number our days

PSALM 91

God is my refuge and my fortress

PSALM 103:1–17A

Praise the Lord, O my soul

PSALM 118:5–9

Take refuge in the Lord

PSALM 121

My help comes from the Lord

PSALM 130

Out of the depths I cry to you, O Lord

PSALM 139:1–18

O Lord, you know me

PSALM 145

The Lord is faithful to his promise

PSALM 146

I will praise the Lord all my life

ISAIAH 25:6–9

God will swallow up death forever

ISAIAH 26:1–4,19

Your dead will live

ISAIAH 40:1–11

Comfort, comfort my people

ISAIAH 40:28,29

God gives strength to the weary

ISAIAH 43:1–3A, 25

You are mine, says the Lord

ISAIAH 44:6–8

I am the first and the last

ISAIAH 55:1–3,6–13

Come, all you who are thirsty

ISAIAH 57:1,2

The righteous find rest

ISAIAH 61:1–3,10,11

Comfort for all who mourn

ISAIAH 65:17–25

New heavens and a new earth

MICAH 6:8

Walk humbly with your God

LAMENTATIONS 3:19–26,31–33,55–57

His compassion never fails

DANIEL 12:1–3

Multitudes who sleep will awake

HOSEA 6:1

Let us return to the Lord

MATTHEW 5:1–12

Blest are the poor in spirit

MATTHEW 6:25–34

Do not worry

MATTHEW 11:28–30

Come to me, all you who are weary

MATTHEW 18:1–5,10

The greatest in the kingdom of heaven

MATTHEW 25:1–13

Wise and foolish

MATTHEW 25:31–46

Take your inheritance

MARK 5:35

Not dead, but asleep

MARK 16:1–8

Jesus' resurrection

MARK 10:13–16

Let the little children come to me

LUKE 7:11–17

Young man, I say to you, get up

LUKE 23:33,39–43

Today you will be with me in paradise

JOHN 3:16–21

God so loved the world

JOHN 5:24–29

The dead will hear his voice and come out

JOHN 6:35–40

I will raise them up on the last day

JOHN 6:47–58

He who believes will have everlasting life

JOHN 10:11–16

I am the Good Shepherd

JOHN 10:27–29

My sheep listen to my voice

JOHN 11:3–4

The one you love is sick

JOHN 11:17-27
I am the resurrection and the life

JOHN 11:38-44
Lazarus, come out

JOHN 14:1-6, 25-27
Do not let your hearts be troubled

JOHN 20:1-18
Jesus' resurrection

ROMANS 5:1-11
Rejoice in the hope of the glory of God

ROMANS 6:3-10
Baptized into Christ's death, raised to life

ROMANS 8:14-24A
Heirs of God

ROMANS 8:28-39
Chosen for salvation

ROMANS 14:7-9
Whether we live or die, we belong to the Lord

1 CORINTHIANS 15:3-8,12-20
Christ died and rose again

1 CORINTHIANS 15:20-24
In Christ shall all be made alive

1 CORINTHIANS 15:35-44
Sown in dishonor, raised in glory

1 CORINTHIANS 15:50-58
Death is swallowed up in victory

2 CORINTHIANS 1:3-5
The God of all comfort

2 CORINTHIANS 4:16—5:1
What is seen is temporary, unseen is eternal

2 CORINTHIANS 5:1-10
Away from the body and at home with the Lord

EPHESIANS 1:3-8
Chosen in Christ

EPHESIANS 2:3-10
Saved through faith

PHILIPPIANS 3:7-14
Know Christ and the power of his resurrection

PHILIPPIANS 3:20-21
Our citizenship is in heaven

COLOSSIANS 3:12-17

Let the peace of Christ rule in your hearts

1 THESSALONIANS 4:13-18

The dead in Christ will rise first

2 TIMOTHY 2:8-13

If we died with him, we will also live with him

HEBREWS 2:14-18

Christ also suffered

HEBREWS 10:35-38

Do not throw away your confidence

HEBREWS 11:1-3,13-16

Aliens and strangers on earth

HEBREWS 12:1-3

Let us fix our eyes on Jesus

JAMES 5:14-16

Confess your sins and pray for each other

1 PETER 1:3-9

A living hope through Christ's resurrection

1 PETER 5:6-11

Cast all your anxiety on him

1 JOHN 3:1-3

Now we are children of God

REVELATION 7:9-17

Standing before the throne in front of the Lamb

REVELATION 14:6,7,12-13

Blessed are the dead who die in the Lord

REVELATION 21:1-4,22-25

A new heaven and a new earth

REVELATION 22:1-5

The Lord will give them light

BIBLIOGRAPHY

On Caregiving

Earl A. Grollman. *Caring and Coping: When Your Loved One Is Seriously Ill.* Boston: Beacon Press, 1995.

James E. Miller. *The Caregiver's Book: Caring for Another, Caring for Yourself.* Minneapolis: Augsburg, 1996.

On Death and Dying

Patricia Anderson. *Affairs in Order.* New York: Macmillan, 1991.

Arthur Byrock. *Dying Well: The Prospect for Growth at the End of Life.* New York: Thorndike, 1997.

Marie de Hennezel. *Intimate Death: How the Dying Teach Us to Live.* New York: Knopf, 1998.

Jan Godfrey. *The Cherry Blossom Tree: A Granfather Talks about Life and Death.* Minneapolis: Augsburg, 1996.

Elizabeth Kübler-Ross. *Questions and Answers on Death and Dying.* New York: Macmillan, 1993.

Jill Westberg McNamara. *My Mom Is Dying: A Child's Diary.* Minneapolis: Augsburg, 1994.

Sherwin Nuland. *How We Die: Reflections on Life's Final Chapter.* New York: Random, 1995.

Timothy Quill. *A Midwife through the Dying Process: Stories of Healing and of Hard Choices at the End of Life.* Baltimore: Johns Hopkins, 1996.

Jack Rieman. *Jewish Insights on Death and Mourning.* New York: Schocken, 1996.

On Grief and Mourning

Theresa Huntley. *Helping Children Grieve: When Someone They Love Dies.* Minneapolis: Augsburg, 1991.

James. E. Miller. *Winter Grief, Summer Grace.* Minneapolis: Augsburg, 1995.

Harold Ivan Smith. *Grieving the Death of a Friend.* Minneapolis: Augsburg, 1996.

Merton P. and A. Irene Strommen. *Five Cries of Grief: One Family's Journey to Healing After the Tragic Death of a Son.* Minneapolis: Augsburg, 1996.

Granger E. Westberg. *Good Grief.* Minneapolis: Fortress Press, 1997.